Dilemmas and Decision Making in Policing

Acknowledgements

The authors would like to thank Julia and Lily at Critical Publishing for their encouragement, patience and guidance.

Emma would also like to acknowledge the ongoing support of her husband Ady and parents Barbara and Brian.

Bob would like to give a special thank you to his wife Tania and daughters Emily and Eve for their unending patience and support.

Dilemmas and Decision Making in Policing

Emma Spooner and Bob Cooper

Routledge
Taylor & Francis Group

LONDON AND NEW YORK

First published in 2023 by Critical Publishing Ltd.

Published 2025 by Routledge
4 Park Square, Milton Park, Abingdon, Oxon OX14 4RN
605 Third Avenue, New York, NY 10017

Routledge is an imprint of the Taylor & Francis Group, an informa business

British Library Cataloguing in Publication Data
A CIP record for this book is available from the British Library

ISBN: 9781041055112 (hbk)
ISBN: 9781915713124 (pbk)
ISBN: 9781041055129 (ebk)

The rights of Bob Cooper and Emma Spooner to be identified as the Authors of this work have been asserted by them in accordance with the Copyright, Design and Patents Act 1988.

Text and cover design by Out of House Limited

DOI: 10.4324/9781041055129

Contents

About the authors

Emma Spooner is a lecturer at the University of Sunderland delivering work-based learning programmes to practitioners involved in investigative practice and policing. She draws on 21 years of policing experience as a frontline practitioner working across the spectrum of volume and priority crime, serious and complex crime and major crime investigation to help to demystify the research process and contextualise it into daily working practices. Helping students to embrace research and understand its application to professional practice and workplace development lies at the heart of her teaching.

Bob Cooper was a detective for 25 years. During that time, he worked as a mentor to his colleagues and delivered numerous training events to both internal and external parties around aspects of investigative practice including decision making. He has a passion for understanding investigative decision making and has used this to underpin discussions with frontline colleagues to help them to develop and maintain standards within the workplace.

Introduction

As a member of the police service, you are operating in an area of increasing diversity and complexity of communities and policing. The National Police Chiefs' Council Policing Vision 2025 emphasises the importance of recruiting and retaining *'confident professionals [who are] able to operate with a high degree of autonomy and accountability and will better reflect its communities'* (NPCC, 2015, p 3). This book supports your development as a professional through encouraging you to be a *thinking investigator*.

You will be working in a messy uncertain world a lot of the time. Rarely will there be only one clear path that neatly presents itself when responding to, or investigating, incidents. Because your work involves people, their emotions and behaviours, things are often unpredictable and complex. Therefore, it is important that you develop your decision-making skills in the face of choice and uncertainty.

Decision making is a core skill and is needed at every level of investigative practice. Embedding good decision-making skills at an early stage of your career will support your growth and development as an investigator. It is for this reason that this book specifically explores decision making from the perspective of the PIP1 volume and priority crime investigator.

Purpose of the book and contents

This book can be used by new police officers or investigators and student officers to explore their experiences as they emerge. It is also useful for anyone in a training role, whether a lecturer, force trainer, tutor or mentor as the scenarios are intended to promote discussion and guided learning. It is also a good refresher for more experienced investigators to reflect on and challenge their own experiences and practices.

The book presents a series of scenarios drawn from real-world policing experiences. The scenarios explore the dilemmas you may be faced with and the decisions you have to make. Within policing the national decision model is the approved approach to decision making (College of Policing, 2013). It consists of a five-step process:

1. gather information and intelligence;

2. assess threat and risk and develop a working strategy;

3. consider powers and policies;

4. identify options and contingencies;

5. take action and review what happened.

The Code of Ethics lies at the heart of the model and you are expected to consider this at every stage. This means that you *'do the right thing in the right way'* (College of Policing, 2014, p 3). The Code of

Ethics provides the principles to guide your decisions and also the standards of professional behaviour that you are expected to employ when making a decision and engaging with the public.

The book consists of seven chapters split into three parts exploring different aspects of policing:

• Part 1 – Policing by consent: decision making and public accountability;

• Part 2 – Managing risk and safeguarding: complex decision making;

• Part 3 – Mindset, choices and priorities: investigative decision making.

The three parts encourage you to move from considering the role of policing in society and how decision making can impact on its legitimacy, to perceptions of risk and safeguarding within investigations, through to operational investigative decision making. However, each of the chapters can also be accessed and utilised as a free-standing source of information and you do not need to read the chapters in order.

Each chapter focuses on specific dilemmas or decisions within the scenario. It guides you through the decisions and your differing options. It draws on policy, guidance and wider research to help inform your decision making. You are encouraged to explore your thinking to help you understand yourself and the decision-making process better and you will be encouraged to critically self-reflect throughout. This reflection can help you to make considered decisions, understanding not only what you are doing but also why you are doing it.

We hope you enjoy working through the book and that it stimulates deeper thought, discussion and more robust and reasoned decision making.

Emma Spooner and Bob Cooper

Part 1

Policing by consent:
decision making and public accountability

Chapter 1
Legitimacy and control: stop and search

Learning objectives

By the end of this chapter you should be able to:

• explain how your decisions impact on the perceived legitimacy of policing;

• explain the potential impact of your decisions on diverse communities;

• identify some of the factors that influence your decision making;

• apply the national decision model to support ethical and reasoned decision making.

Introduction

This chapter explores how you exercise your powers of stop and search. This power is most often used for searching people for controlled drugs (Nickolls and Allen, 2022). However, the principles discussed are equally applicable to searches you may conduct for other items or purposes.

The chapter uses a fictional scenario to explore your thinking. You are encouraged to consider your stance on the role of stop and search by examining your values and your views on the role of the police in society. You will explore your own identity to understand how it influences the decisions you make.

Finally, the chapter considers how to make reasoned and robust decisions by exploring the national decision model. It discusses not only how to make decisions to maximise the chance of a positive outcome, but also how to convey your decision to others to increase the perception of fairness of the process.

Scenario

Stop and search

I was on patrol with my tutor this evening when we saw a black man aged in his early 20s standing in the street by an alleyway. He looked towards us several times and appeared nervous. My tutor said he had previously cautioned him for possession of cannabis. He asked me if I thought we should stop and search him.

$\longrightarrow$

I am aware that the estate that we were driving through is a high-crime area, notorious for drug dealing and knife crime. From my experience, a lot of the violent crime involves young black men as both victims and suspects. I have also heard my colleagues refer to this area as being a problem estate. They speak about the importance of asserting our authority and getting in their faces.

Usually, there is some discussion in the briefing about how many searches were conducted the previous day. I feel embarrassed if I have nothing to report and I am worried what the rest of the shift think of me and whether they think I am being lazy or just not up to the job.

However, it was made really clear during my training that to conduct a stop and search I need to have the grounds to do so. I am aware that it can cause problems with the community. However, I also remember a briefing last week where the inspector was talking about a rise in knife violence linked to gangs and drug dealing and how tackling it was a priority for us.

My tutor then added he had seen an intelligence report stating that a man matching his description was regularly dealing drugs from this area so we would stop and search him. I started to talk to the man, but he immediately became angry. I raised my voice to be heard over him, repeatedly telling him to calm down. He started swearing, saying that he had been stopped three times so far this year and accused us of being racist. I felt annoyed as I am not racist, and I am just trying to do my job. His comment upset me and made me angry that I should be accused of this. I started to wonder whether he was behaving like this because he was trying to hide something.

My tutor then stepped in and explained clearly and calmly why we had stopped him and engaged with him to provide a lot of information. He presented the grounds for the search in a really clear way and he sounded fair and balanced. I liked the way my tutor behaved with the man; I could see what a positive impact he was having on the encounter and I liked his pace and style of talking – he was non-threatening and just took his time. After a few minutes, the man did calm down and I was then able to search him. Nothing was found.

I still wonder whether it was the right decision to stop him. Surely if someone has nothing to hide then they will understand that I am just trying to do my job and make the community safer. But then I wonder how I would feel if I kept getting stopped when I knew I hadn't done anything wrong. But as a police officer, how can I tackle crime if I don't stop and search people? I feel like I am caught between a rock and a hard place.

You might have some strong opinions about this scenario and about the use of stop and search. You may agree or disagree with some of the reflections the officer makes. The rest of this chapter examines your reactions, exploring how you think and how it impacts on your decision making and your actions.

The legitimacy of policing

Stop and search can be a controversial subject. You are encouraged to approach this chapter with an open mind and explore the differing viewpoints to develop a balanced approach to support you in utilising the power most effectively.

The use of stop and search has been linked to creating mistrust with individuals and within communities. Therefore, this section briefly examines the history of stop and search and its impact on the relationship between the police and public.

History of stop and search

Historically, the police had powers to stop and search if they suspected someone may be planning to carry out a crime under what were known as the *sus laws*. However, justification for the searches was sometimes weak.

Throughout the 1970s, this contributed to poor relations with the black population with criticisms of racial profiling and unfair policing tactics being used on black communities. In 1981, the Metropolitan Police launched Operation Swamp, leading to about 1,000 people being stopped and searched. This further increased tension and was one of the catalysts for the Brixton riots, exposing the divisions between the police and the communities they served.

Following the riots, a review highlighted the disadvantages that the black population were facing (Scarman, 1981). It identified issues with confidence and trust in the police and poor community liaison. The sus laws were abolished and the Police and Criminal Evidence Act (PACE) 1984 was introduced, more clearly defining the stop and search powers of the police. The accompanying Codes of Practice set the procedures and rules for the police to follow when conducting any stop and search.

By 2009, approximately 1.5 million stop and searches were being conducted annually, but there were criticisms that it continued to be used unfairly and in a discriminatory manner. In light of these criticisms, tighter restrictions were placed on the use of stop and search. This decreased searches to about 279,000 in 2018. However, more recent times have seen a resurgence of stop and search as a response to rising violent crime (Nickolls and Allen, 2022).

Stop and search is deeply embedded in black history. It is important as a police officer that you understand these tensions as they continue to affect police and community relations. Historic mistrust and resentment echo in modern-day encounters. However, this is not just an historic issue. It is a very real present-day issue with black people and those from a minority ethnic background being disproportionately represented within the stop and search figures year after year (HMICFRS, 2021a).

Much of the literature discusses stop and search in relation to racial tensions and disproportionate use against black communities. However, the issues around decision making and engagement with the public are as relevant for all individuals subjected to a stop and search.

The problems with stop and search

Some of the main issues with stop and search have been highlighted as:

- *weak grounds;*
- *decision-making influenced by bias;*
- *inappropriate communication;*
- *excessive force.*

(IOPC, 2022a)

It has been identified that the police have a lack of understanding of the impact of disproportionate searches on black people and why their actions may be seen as discriminatory (HMICFRS, 2021a). It is recognised that unfair or poorly targeted searches can increase mistrust and decrease confidence in the police (Nickolls and Allen, 2022).

It must be recognised that stop and search, when used correctly, is a powerful tool. However, you should understand the impact of using this power on policing in a wider social context.

Legitimacy

Stop and search has been linked to questions about the legitimacy of policing, which strikes at the core principle of *policing by consent*.

While in some countries the police are used as an extension of the state to impose order, the UK relies on public co-operation and willing compliance. People feel a responsibility to follow the rules. This is the essence of legitimacy. Complete the following exercise to start developing your understanding of legitimacy.

Explore your thinking

In 2022, the government was embroiled in *Partygate*. This revolved around parties that were held at Downing Street while the UK was subject to Covid-19 restrictions, resulting in a number of fines being issued for breach of lockdown conditions.

- Spend a few minutes thinking about how you felt about the Prime Minister, the government and the wider political landscape at that time.
- Consider what your family, friends, colleagues or the media were saying.
- Note down a few words that immediately come to mind.

You may have noted words such as disappointed, disillusioned or even anger, perhaps disinterest, indifference or apathy.

Whether you personally felt there was any wrongdoing or not, for some the behaviours eroded trust. When those in authority are perceived to act in a way that disregards their own rules, it can lead to people questioning their legitimacy. This can result in people becoming distrustful, disinterested and ultimately disengaged.

Legitimacy is a quality that an authority holds that *'leads others to feel obligated to obey its decisions and directives'* (Tyler, 2003, p 308). Legitimacy is important for institutions that possess a position of authority over the public, including the police, and is vital for policing by consent.

The police need people to follow directions when given and also to support the flow of information in investigations. A lack of perceived legitimacy in policing can lead to dissatisfaction, resentment and legal cynicism. This can cause a loss of trust, people feeling marginalised and excluded from society, and it can hinder co-operation and compliance (Jackson et al, 2012). When there is a perception that stop and search is being used unfairly, it evokes this response and erodes legitimacy, undermining policing by consent. Legitimacy in policing is about transparent and ethical decision making and demonstrating the application of your powers fairly.

Procedural justice

Researchers have put forward the notion that one way of achieving legitimacy is through procedural justice (see Tyler, 2003 for a full discussion). This focuses on behaving in a manner that engenders trust. One way to build trust is by acting fairly. Complete the following exercise to explore why being seen to be fair is important.

Explore your thinking

Think about an experience where you feel you have been treated unfairly by someone in authority, eg a schoolteacher, parent/caregiver, supervisor.

• Write down a couple of words about how it made you feel.

Now think about a situation where you feel you have been treated fairly by a person in authority.

• Again, write down a few words about how that made you feel.

It is likely that you have recorded negative words in relation to the unfair example and positive feelings in relation to the fair example.

• What did the person do that made their actions seem unfair or fair?

• How did that make you feel about them?

Their actions likely impacted on your feelings, your sense of fairness and ultimately perhaps your belief in their legitimacy, their right to exert power over you.

Decisions are more likely to be considered fair when they are neutral, unbiased and objective (Tyler, 2003). In stop and search, being open, respectful and transparent when engaging with people allows you to demonstrate the objectivity of your decision making (HMICFRS, 2021a). Therefore, the quality of your decision making is fundamental to procedural justice.

This chapter revisits this concept later to discuss how you put procedural justice into practice. First, though, you need to understand what influences the way you make decisions to help minimise bias and support objectivity in your decision making.

Understanding your decision making

This section explores how your values, biases and identity may impact your decision making.

Values

In policing, values such as trust, honesty, integrity and justice may be important to you. The following exercise encourages you to think about one of those values, justice, to see how it may affect the way you police.

Explore your thinking

Spend a few minutes thinking about what *justice* means to you and your beliefs about how justice should be done.

• Do you think crime control is more important than individual rights?

• Is it okay to override the rights of a suspect in order to achieve a greater good?

These are fundamental issues and the bedrock of the criminal justice system. The following section explores these differences in a little more detail.

A crime control approach would argue that it is better to conduct a high volume of stop and searches in order to reduce or prevent crime. The rights of the individual being subject to those searches are less important than the greater good of protecting the community from harm.

You may still hear your colleagues argue that stop and search is an effective crime control tool, particularly for knife crime. However, only about 2 per cent of searches result in offensive weapons or firearms being found (Home Office, 2022a). Additionally, research has found that stop and search has a minimal deterrent effect but instead is sometimes used as a way of asserting authority and power (Tiratelli et al, 2018).

Historically, a crime control approach was adopted in policing. However, this approach led to miscarriages of justice as individual rights were neglected. The introduction of PACE saw a shift from crime control towards due process and a criminal justice system that protects individuals from undue coercion or oppression while following clearly defined rules and procedures. It is intended to try to balance the rights of the community to justice with the rights of individuals who are suspected of crime.

This can be quite complex to understand, so think about a situation that may feel more familiar to you. In public health, a problem the authorities had to cope with was the Covid-19 pandemic. Some countries chose to impose very strict lockdown conditions. These measures were aimed at controlling the virus and individual freedoms were of less concern. Other countries tried to reach more of a balance between imposing restrictions to achieve some control of the virus while still recognising individual rights and therefore conditions were not as strict. The question to consider is which is the better option: control of the virus but with fewer rights for the individual, or a little less control of the virus but more rights for individuals?

If you apply this to policing, then the problem that the police are trying to control is crime. Do you adopt the crime control model where the focus is all about reducing and preventing crime, and individual rights and freedoms are less important? Or do you try to achieve a balance between tackling crime while also protecting the rights of all individuals?

These are complex questions, but UK policing adopts the balance shown in a due process approach. This doesn't mean shying away from your core responsibilities of the prevention and detection of crime but there is a balance to be met. The rights of individuals have to be respected at all stages and processes lawfully applied when exercising your powers.

Stereotyping

Decision making needs to be unbiased and objective. However, sometimes decisions can be skewed by our personal biases, but it is not always easy to recognise them as they are often subconscious, automatic and can feel quite intuitive. This section explores one of those biases – stereotyping.

Within policing this is a powerful process that you need to be aware of to challenge your thinking and some of the automatic stereotypes you may unwittingly apply. Informally, you may hear your colleagues say that in their experience some ethnic groups are mainly responsible for some types of crime. However, you should critically assess this claim. Statistical analysis is problematic as over-policing of some ethnicities may result in over-representation in some crime types, creating a false impression. Even if a link could definitively be proved then you should still not be using racial profiling to justify searches. This is discriminatory and unacceptable behaviour.

One of the problems with stereotypes is that people tend to live up, or down, to our expectations of them. Black people are eight times more likely to be handcuffed while compliant than white people during a stop and search (HMICFRS, 2021a). Research has shown that 'stereotypical perceptions of Black people as dangerous, violent, volatile, and having "superhuman" strength may be contributing to the disproportionate use of force and restraint against such individuals' (Open Society Foundations, 2019 and Angiolini, 2017, cited in IOPC, 2022a, p 23).

If you associate certain characteristics and anticipate behaviours, then you interpret information to support that belief. So, if you are anticipating aggression and non-compliance then when the person expresses their frustration, this is easier to interpret in line with your preconceived expectations.

Sometimes during stop and search encounters, you will be faced with accusations of racism. This can feel confronting and may make you feel upset or angry that you are being challenged in this way. Be aware that emotions can impact your decision making and when people are angry, they tend to make quicker decisions, relying more on automatic processing such as stereotyping rather than making objective decisions. Recognising and being able to manage your emotions is an important skill to develop as a police officer and will help you to remain more objective.

Organisational culture, socialisation and conformity

Within stop and search, research has indicated that aspects of negative police culture can impact on interactions. People report that the police can be accusatory, unbelieving, adopt a guilty until proven innocent attitude, and try to assert their authority. This goes against the principles of procedural justice and can be problematic within stop and search encounters.

When you join a new organisation, you will often go through a period of socialisation where you learn not only the formal rules and knowledge, but are also socialised into the informal rules, processes and procedures. In general, people want to fit in with the group and be accepted. If newcomers don't abide by the informal rules and the accepted way of behaving, then they risk social exclusion and rejection. You may therefore be at risk of feeling a social pressure to conform with some of the more negative cultural attitudes and behaviours as you are socialised into policing, so it is valuable to spend time reflecting on your own ideas of professionalism and your own identity.

Professional identity

Complete the following exercise to help you start applying this concept to yourself.

Explore your thinking

- What behaviours do you think make a professional?
- What characteristics do you associate with a police officer?
- What characteristics do you want to embody, ie who do you want to be?
- How do you want others to see you?

This starts to give you an idea of what is important to you and how you want to behave. You will develop your identity as you progress as a police officer. As a young in-service officer you will have the opportunity to work with lots of different people. You should use this as a chance to observe and see what works well and what you feel comfortable with. In the earlier scenario, the officer expressed her preference for the calm and explanatory manner used by the tutor. She could learn from this and try to adopt this into her own style.

When starting a new career, you may be trialling different identities and trying to fit in with what you think others expect of you. Stone and Pettigrew (2000) reported negative attitudes that officers demonstrated, including being cocky, patronising, arrogant, intimidating, sarcastic, using offensive language, and being directive and accusatory. Are these characteristics you would want to be associated with?

Furthermore, they found that stop and search encounters are more positive when the officer is polite, pleasant, friendly, enquiring and helpful. As a police officer, you should be able to manage hostility without resorting to counter-productive behaviours that may serve to enflame a situation.

Understanding yourself is the first step to understanding your approach to dilemmas and decision making.

How to make reasoned decisions

This section explores the practicalities of making a decision. There are two parts to decision making in policing: making the decision and then conveying that decision. These two aspects will be explored to help you develop your reasoned decision-making skills.

How do you make the decision?

This section applies the national decision model (College of Policing, 2013) to the earlier stop and search scenario.

Gather information and intelligence

The starting point for any decision is to ensure you have as much information as is reasonably possible. You should consider the strength and reliability of any information too.

Explore your thinking

Consider the scenario at the start of this chapter.

• Do you feel that you had enough information to make an informed decision?

• What other information do you want?

– What does *'looking nervous'* mean?

– Is the intelligence current and accurate?

– What is the physical description from the intelligence?

– Does the intelligence give more specific timings or location?

Think critically about the information you are taking in and avoid making assumptions. Try to gather as much information as possible that may develop or negate your suspicion, for example does he appear to be trying to conceal something, did you see him drop anything, did you observe him interacting with anyone beforehand and handing over or receiving items etc?

Assess threat and risk and develop a working strategy

It is clear that you need to consider your own safety in any stop and search. However, this stage also asks you to go further and to assess the wider situation, considering the potential for harm to be caused and the wider impact on community relations.

You should be familiar with your force priorities as they will dictate where the organisation sees the threat, harm and risk and wants you to focus your efforts. As evidence-based practitioners, you should consider whether the targeting of offences such as simple possession of cannabis is the best use of limited time and resources or would it be better spent engaging in more focused and targeted searches and gathering intelligence and information? This book does not seek to answer these questions as this matter is one for a wider debate on policing, but it does encourage you to think critically about these issues. High levels of stop and search for low level drug possession with weak grounds may be more harmful and the damage to police community relations may outweigh the benefits (HMICFRS, 2021a).

You are not encouraged to ignore criminal behaviour but to consider what you are actually seeing and whether you have the genuine grounds to undertake a search, weighing up the risk and benefits in their widest sense. This asks you to consider the necessity and proportionality of any search as well as the legality of it.

Consider powers and policies

Whenever you make a decision, you need to draw on the legislation and any policies and guidance. For stop and search the following are fundamental:

• PACE Codes of Practice A;

• College of Policing Authorised Professional Practice.

You also need to be aware of the associated legislation for stop and search (eg section 23 of the Misuse of Drugs Act 1971). You may also have local policies and guidance documents to provide additional support. You need to familiarise yourself with these documents as they should underpin your decisions.

In order to utilise your powers of stop and search, you need to have *reasonable grounds to suspect*. You may recognise this phrase from your power of arrest under section 24 of PACE 1984. Your powers of stop and search are an alternative to arrest. It is a power that allows you to investigate immediately in order to *allay or confirm* your suspicions without having to go through the full arrest process. The use of the term *reasonable grounds to suspect* as a prerequisite for arrest and stop and search indicates that a similar level of suspicion is required for both (HMICFRS, 2021a).

Within stop and search, reasonable grounds to suspect means that you must have a genuine suspicion that you will find the object that is being searched for. That suspicion needs to be based on objective factors. If someone else was presented with the same information, then they would be able to reach the same conclusions. Objective grounds can never be intuition, a gut feeling or instinct as they are subjective (individual to you) rather than objective.

Some criteria are specifically excluded from being considered as grounds for the search. These include, but are not limited to, previous convictions, stereotypical beliefs about certain groups of people being involved in criminality, or physical appearance (unless the person fits a description that has been provided). PACE Code A provides more detail about excluded criteria and you need to be aware of these. These criteria can never be used, either alone or in combination with any other factors, to justify a search.

A range of grounds is better than a single one so try to build a collage of objective factors. These may include accurate and reliable intelligence or information, and observations about specific behaviour. You can overlay this against the location and time of day if appropriate too.

Therefore, you can see that there may be some grounds that could support the search in the earlier scenario (eg looking nervous, time, location, intelligence report) but they would need further explanation and justification to make them stronger. The man's ethnicity and previous caution cannot form any part of the grounds for search. Whichever factors you rely upon, you need to be able to articulate them and justify them; if you cannot do this, then you should not be conducting the search.

Identify options and contingencies

In this stage of the model, you identify what your choices are based upon your assessment so far. As a police officer you have discretion, so you can use your judgement to decide on the most appropriate course of action of those that you identify. Within the scenario outlined, there are several options including the following.

• Do nothing and continue the patrol.

• Stop and talk to the man. If you do not feel you have reasonable grounds, then you are still allowed to speak to the man. This is *not* a stop and search and you have no power to detain the person or make them speak to you.

• Stop and search the man if you have the grounds and you consider it proportionate. You can engage in a conversation beforehand, and you can also ask questions which might negate the need for a search.

There are lots of alternatives you could also consider either in isolation or in combination with the above such as re-patrolling after a set period of time to see if the person is still there and whether their continued presence raises suspicions. You may consider submitting an intelligence report depending on what you have observed. You may wish to undertake more intelligence checks to develop a better understanding of the crime patterns and information about the specific location to allow you to conduct more targeted patrols at another time.

Always consider your contingencies too; for example, there is a possibility that as soon as you engage with the man, he, or an onlooker, may start recording the encounter – how would you deal with that? Consider the potential outcomes so you can be prepared to deal with them.

Take action and review what happened

Having arrived at your decision, you then need to implement it and the practicalities of conducting the search will be discussed in the next section. The review part of the model means that you should assess what happened and the outcomes. This does not just involve reviewing the actual actions you took; instead, take the time to reflect on your choices and behaviours and understand what was driving your decision making. Reflective practice is vital because decision making on the street can be quick and instinctive. Reflection allows you to explore your decisions more slowly to understand them better and challenge your thinking where necessary. This can help you to continue to develop as a professional.

How do you implement the decision?

Being able to convey the rationale for the decision can be as important as the decision itself. A fundamental part of procedural justice is the public being able to see that there is fair decision making. Complaints about stop and search often centre on the lack of grounds provided or a belief that the search is being conducted due to assumptions made by the officer rather than objective grounds. Therefore, conveying this information clearly can really support your decision making.

Providing information about the grounds for the decision can help to support the person's compliance. Having an explanation can help one person to understand another person's actions and to minimise the risk of them making assumptions about what is happening.

Within stop and search, the mnemonic GOWISELY is used to provide the person being searched with information. It is not intended within this book to revisit the stages of that model as it is well discussed by the College of Policing. However, GOWISELY is not always communicated or recorded (IOPC, 2022a). If you are struggling or reluctant to explain, then you should be asking yourself whether you should actually be doing the search.

Another concern that sometimes arises with stop and search encounters is the attitude of the police officer. Remember the principles of procedural justice. Make sure you act with professionalism and fairness; try and use your informal communication skills to convey what you are doing and why you are doing it so the person can understand. Be respectful and courteous, treat people with dignity and try to be polite. There is no place for rudeness, sarcasm or inappropriate jokes. People may be experiencing a range of emotions including feeling 'victimised, humiliated and violated' (IOPC, 2022a, p 35), as well as frustrated, confused or angry (HMICFRS, 2021a). As a professional police officer, you should be able to use your skills to recognise some of these emotional cues and to adapt your communication to manage these situations to try to seek co-operation in the first instance.

If you need to use force then ensure you are able to justify it, rather than it being a routine action or because you haven't taken the time to try to develop a rapport. Of course, some people will never react well no matter how calm and professional you are and how well supported your decision making is, but that does not mean that you should not make genuine efforts to try.

As well as verbally explaining your decision and the grounds, you must also complete the stop and search form. This is your opportunity to accurately and fully document your decision and the grounds you used to support your action. The College of Policing also recommends using body-worn video as early as possible, including in the lead-up to the stop and search to capture behaviours that support your decision making.

Evidence-based policing and stop and search

The evidence base would suggest that searches are more effective when there are stronger grounds to support them. An HMICFRS (2021a) study reviewed 9378 stop and search records and found the following:

• 21 per cent had strongly recorded grounds and these resulted in a 40 per cent find rate;

• 42 per cent had moderate recorded grounds and these resulted in a 22 per cent find rate;

• 22 per cent had weak recorded grounds and these resulted in a 17 per cent find rate;

• 14 per cent did not have reasonable grounds and these resulted in a 14 per cent find rate.

Strong grounds can also increase the perception that the search is fair and reasonable.

Stop and search is often cited as a vital tool in the fight against serious crime and knife crime. Only about 11 per cent of stop and searches result in an arrest (Home Office, 2022a). Over two-thirds of stop and searches relate to drugs (Nickolls and Allen, 2022) and it is estimated that half of the searches are for possession only despite this rarely being a force priority (HMICFRS, 2021a). There is little evidence to support the notion that stop and search has a significant crime control effect and it has been suggested that rather than thinking of it as a crime reduction tactic, it should be better seen as an investigative tool for individual situations (Tiratelli et al, 2018).

To tackle serious and violent crime, policing needs accurate and reliable intelligence and public co-operation. This is reliant on community engagement and willingness to support the police. Poorly targeted and conducted stop and search erodes trust, compliance and co-operation and makes people less willing to engage in the criminal justice process.

This is not about risk-averse decision making. This chapter is not encouraging you to avoid conducting a stop and search; it is encouraging you to conduct more focused searches with stronger objective grounds. It is asking you to behave professionally and respectfully. The national decision model provides you with the bedrock of sound informed decision making where you understand what you are doing and why. By acting in a way that maximises compliance and co-operation, not only can you contribute to police legitimacy, but it can make your job that little bit easier too.

Key points

The main things for you to remember to help you make informed decisions about stop and search are:

• most stop and searches result in nothing being recovered;

• stop and search is an alternative to arrest so similar levels of suspicion should be present;

• people need to understand why they are being stopped and searched;

• people want to feel they are being treated fairly and with dignity and courtesy;

• decision making is considered fairer when it is consistent, rule-based and unbiased;

• the national decision model can support your decision making.

Further reading

The College of Policing Authorised Professional Practice site has further essential reading to help you understand how to properly use your powers of stop and search:
www.college.police.uk/app/stop-and-search/stop-and-search

For more information on stop and search powers in relation to section 60, terrorism, and Serious Violence Reduction Order, see Nickolls and Allen (2022).

Chapter 2
The role of the police: policing protests and demonstrations

Learning objectives

By the end of this chapter you should be able to:

- explain the importance of protests within a human rights framework;
- understand the role of the police in policing protests;
- recognise your own worldview towards protests and how that may affect your behaviours;
- apply the principles of legality, proportionality and necessity to inform your decision making in a protest-related incident.

Introduction

This chapter explores your responsibilities while policing protests. It situates this within a human rights framework, recognising the role the police have to play in promoting rights for all parties and the conflicts that this can sometimes bring. It examines the role of the police, particularly focusing on the need for impartiality and independence.

It explores your own thoughts on protests and protestors and how your worldview can impact your decisions and actions. The chapter applies the principles of legality, proportionality and necessity to help you make reasoned and informed decisions. Finally, it explores the importance of your communication skills and how these can help you to manage potential sources of conflict.

While the overall strategy and direction of policing a protest will be set at a more senior level, you need to consider your own decision making within these events and how you meet the right balance in your response on the ground.

Scenario

I had my rest days cancelled last week as there was a protest that was taking place. I attended a large briefing where we were advised about what was happening and were allocated our duties. The protest was part of the Black Lives Matter movement, which

→

I think is a really important cause. When I reached the area that I was responsible for policing there was a large crowd. They were good-natured and seemed to be in good spirits. I was chatting to them about the issues and why they felt the need to come and protest. One member of the group then made a speech rallying the others around him. People in the crowd then started to take the knee to show their support for their cause. Some of those closest to me were asking me to join them. I felt that as this is such an important issue for equality, it would be wrong for me not to show solidarity, so I did kneel for a short period of time. A couple of my colleagues did the same, but others remained standing and I'm not sure if I did the right thing or not.

Later in the afternoon, a couple of local residents came up to me to complain about the protest and the disruption it was causing them. They started shouting at the protestors and were threatening to drive their car into the crowd, who had spilled on to the road, to make them move. I then felt caught between protecting the protestors and supporting the local community and whose rights were more important. A couple of the protestors were refusing to move and kept quoting case law at me, which made me a little unsure of my powers. However, after some time, we managed to persuade most of them to clear the road so that traffic could pass while they could still gather in the pedestrian areas.

As the evening wore on, we were called to another area where some minor disorder had broken out. There were hundreds of people milling about and I saw a large group gathering around a statue of a prominent local historical figure. I am aware the statue of the man has attracted controversy previously due to his involvement in the slave trade. I saw several people urinating on it and I needed to make a decision as to whether I would challenge them or not. I spoke to my colleagues and we decided not to intervene as the crowd was very large and seemed to be growing more aggressive.

The following day I saw reports on the local news and on social media where the police were being criticised for the way they handled the protests. It is hard to please everyone and while I received some basic public order training during my initial training, I am not in a specialist role and had never policed a protest before so at times I was unsure of what I should be doing for the best.

Explore your thinking

Think about how you would have reacted in that situation. Consider the following questions.

• What are your thoughts about protests and protestors?

• Do you understand why people protest?

- Would you engage in an act of solidarity?
- Whose rights do you think are more important: those of the protestors or the people affected by the protest?
- What would you have done if you had witnessed criminal behaviour during the protest?

Policing protests can put you in a difficult position. You have to reach a balance between enabling a lawful protest and taking action when necessary. Often you will be policing under a spotlight of media attention and therefore this chapter helps you to explore your thoughts, knowledge and behaviour to help you make justifiable and defensible decisions under the glare of public scrutiny.

History of protests

To understand the viewpoints of protestors and the policing response to protest, it is helpful to briefly explore its history. This section helps to develop an understanding of what an integral part of a free democratic society protest is, along with how the authorities and protestors have often found themselves in conflict. It explores how the right to protest developed and how the policing response to protests has evolved.

Fighting for rights

The right to protest is a relatively modern phenomenon and part of its value is that it gives people a voice which historically was denied to them. The Peasants' Revolt led by Wat Tyler in 1381 is one of the earliest situations where a popular social movement sought to have its rights recognised. At that time, a new poll tax had been introduced, creating an environment where people became disaffected and angry with the authorities. As a result, Wat Tyler and his followers attacked a number of castles and strongholds and eventually stormed into London causing widespread damage, beheading some of the king's men and forcing the king himself to negotiate (Hethmon, 2020).

At this time there was no right to peaceful protest, so people had no other way to stand up to the authorities and ruling classes. They were powerless to make their views heard other than through rebellion. Think about some of the scenes you see in the media from other countries where criticism of the ruling authorities is discouraged, and protests are quashed, often quickly and violently. Ultimately, what recourse does this leave to people if they can't stand up for their rights in a legitimate manner? This underlines the importance of the right to protest in a democratic society to give people a platform to try to achieve their objectives in a non-violent manner.

There has also been a long history of conflict between protestors and authorities and con-troversy about the tactics used to manage protests. In 1819, against a backdrop of wage cuts and unemployment, a protest was arranged demanding parliamentary reform. The gathering took place at St Peter's Field in Manchester and involved about 60,000 to 100,000 people. Despite local reports at the time saying this was a peaceful protest, the local yeomanry (a volunteer cavalry) were called in to clear the field and reports state they charged with sabres drawn, resulting in between 10 and 20 deaths and many casualties. Blame was split between the yeomanry for being too aggressive with a peaceful meeting, while others said the protestors were being violent (Maher, 2014). Responding with force to protests has always proved controversial and this is no less true today. More recent protests, including those against the poll tax in 1990 and the G20 protests in 2009, have led to criticisms of policing tactics and the level of force used. The need for a proportionate response to protest is critical to maintaining public support.

When peaceful protest appears ineffective, sometimes people have pushed at the boundaries of what is acceptable and turned to violent methods in order to get important issues heard. In the twentieth century, one group advocated deeds not words in order to bring about change. This resulted in them using violent and extreme actions. The movement saw the use of explosives, bombs, arson, physical assault, criminal damage, chemicals being placed in post boxes, attacks on works of art and damaging artefacts at the British Museum (Riddell, 2018). This group were widely disliked, assaulted by members of the public and put under surveillance by special branch (Atkinson, 2018). Would it surprise you to learn that this group was actually the Women's Social and Political Movement, founded in 1903 and headed by Emmeline Pankhurst and her daughters, with the aim of securing the right to vote for women?

History has painted a sympathetic picture of the suffragettes and it is hard to imagine a time when this basic right was not granted to women. Can you see some similarities in some of the actions taken by protest groups now? With modern protests sometimes it can be difficult to understand what they are trying to achieve or how they plan to achieve it. The very ideas themselves can seem alien and unachievable and sometimes undesirable. As the police it is important that you avoid being pulled into the politics of what the protest is about but instead focus on your role of policing them fairly and impartially, upholding the law, maintaining the peace and protecting human rights.

Development of human rights

In 1948, the Universal Declaration of Human Rights was the start of what is now recognised as human rights, aimed at protecting basic rights for people. It paved the way for the European Convention on Human Rights (ECHR) in 1950 of which the UK became a signatory (United Nations, 2022). This established the right to peaceful protest. ECHR was embedded into UK law under the Human Rights Act 1998. Even though the UK has now left the European Union it is still a signatory to ECHR and still abides by the Human Rights Act.

ECHR embeds the right to peaceful protest through freedom of expression and assembly. However, these are not absolute rights, and laws that restrict these rights can be implemented for reasons such as the maintenance of order. Furthermore, the state can interfere with the right to peaceful protest to protect the rights and freedoms of others in certain circumstances. This is where the policing approach to protests can sometimes be more problematic in understanding when that tipping point has been reached, whose rights take precedence and how the police react to it.

Legislation and policing approach

In 2009, London hosted the G20 convention. As is often the case with this event, there were a number of protests. However, the protests turned violent and the police responded with force. During the course of this, a newspaper vendor Ian Tomlinson was struck several times with a baton by a police officer as he tried to make his way home through the streets of London. Mr Tomlinson died shortly afterwards with the subsequent inquest finding that the injuries sustained were the cause of death. The police officer involved was cleared of manslaughter but was found guilty of gross misconduct and was dismissed. There was widespread public and media condemnation about the level of force and tactics used.

It was recognised that a change in the way police managed protests was needed, and as a result a policy of open communication and a presumption of a peaceful protest using force only as a last resort was adopted. However, more recent protests such as those by Extinction Rebellion and Just Stop Oil, which have caused widespread disruption, have led to renewed questioning of policing tactics and whether a more robust approach is required. It was felt that the balance had tipped too far towards the rights of the protestors and was over-riding the rights of the community.

As a response to evolving means of protest and the powers to deal effectively with them, the Conservative government introduced the Police, Crime, Sentencing and Courts Act 2022. Part 3 of the Act deals with public order policing and widens police powers in response to highly disruptive but peaceful protest. It also created a new offence of intentionally or reck- lessly causing public nuisance. The powers are not without controversy and are seen by some as an imposition on human rights.

The problems with policing protests

Peaceful protest is considered a fundamental human right and is arguably an essential part of a tolerant and democratic society. However, as ECHR recognises, it is not an absolute right and sometimes this causes a dilemma as to what action can be taken against protestors and how far that action can or should go. Some key issues and dilemmas that have arisen in rela- tion to policing protests are as follows:

• the appropriateness of engaging in a symbolic act, eg taking the knee;

• knowledge of, and confidence in using, the powers available to the police;

• when to intervene in peaceful but highly disruptive protests;

• balancing whether to ignore or deal with minor offences;

• when to use force and how much to use;

• meeting the right balance between tolerance and enforcement, being too soft or too hard.

Role of the police

In order to understand what you should or should not be doing when policing a protest, it is worth exploring the fundamental role of the police. If you understand your purpose, then it can help you to determine the best course of action and support your decision making. This section therefore examines the principles that underpin policing in the UK and how these can be challenged in protest situations. It also explores how your own ethical stance as an individual can present challenges for you when policing protests.

Impartiality and independence

Chapter 1 explored the importance of the legitimacy of the police. One way that legitimacy can be achieved is through policing demonstrating impartiality and independence from politics. Being seen to be biased or unfairly applying your powers can be harmful to police-public relations and the principle of policing by consent.

Consider the following exercise to start exploring your own views on impartiality and what it means to you as a police officer.

Explore your thinking

Think about the media coverage of some of the Black Lives Matter protests. Protestors adopted a symbolic act of 'taking the knee' to show support and solidarity with the cause. While policing these events, the media showed images of some police officers taking the knee and this was met with a mixed reaction in the media.

• What were your thoughts about the police taking this action?

• Would you have done the same?

• What are your reasons for your response?

• How do you think this action could be perceived?

• If you were policing a far right march and the protestors asked you to make a Nazi salute gesture, would you do this?

It is likely that you were outraged by this last question and of course this is something that you should never do. The point here though is that these two examples are the opposite ends of the spectrum but how do you decide which is appropriate and which is not, especially if you are policing in a greyer area with regards to public perception and where the lines are less clear?

A review by HMICFRS (2021b) recognises the difficulties with decision making about taking a symbolic act. They highlight that the National Police Chiefs' Council issued guidance advising that it was at the discretion of individual officers to decide whether to take the knee based on the circumstances at the time. While some forces abided by this, others issued advice to their officers that such action would be inadvisable. HMICFRS recognise that this is a delicate area and such an action may be actually seen as supporting equality, an important issue. However, they go on to state that when an action becomes synonymous with a cause, then engaging in that act can be seen as showing support for that protest or its aim and they say that this *'will rarely be appropriate'* (HMICFRS, 2021b, p 74).

They do also acknowledge, however, that when the action is taken in a situation where tension or unrest is building, and the act may avert that, then a spur-of-the-moment decision is unlikely to be criticised. This demonstrates the difficult position that officers can find themselves in and the pressures you can face from protestors. The important thing to remember here is to have an awareness of how the action may be perceived, and to truly understand your reasons if you choose to engage in the act. If you are doing it only to show support for the cause, then this is unlikely to be appropriate as it can raise doubt about your impartiality.

As a police officer you undertook an oath to act *'with fairness, integrity, diligence and impartiality, upholding fundamental human rights and according equal respect to all people'* (Police Act 1996 as amended by the Police Reform Act 2002). This basic preposition recognises the conflicting demands that are on police officers and the different directions they can easily find themselves being pulled in. If you start to demonstrate support for some causes through the actions you take, then you may risk compromising your impartiality. It can lead to difficult questions being asked if you choose to partake in a symbolic act in one protest but refuse to in another protest.

Furthermore, the attestation also made you declare *'that I will, to the best of my power, cause the peace to be kept and preserved and prevent all offences against people and property'*. This is your core role; your purpose when policing protests. You are there to protect human rights, keep the peace and prevent harm, and you need to do this fairly and impartially.

An impartial approach across all protests, whether you fundamentally agree with them or not, demonstrates an even-handed approach and a consistency that helps to promote legitimacy in policing.

Beliefs and ethics

In Chapter 1 the role of values in guiding your actions was considered. It is likely that you hold a value of freedom, including freedom of speech, freedom of thought etc; these are things that are probably important to you. However, it is your beliefs and your ethics that will determine your idea of the right way of achieving those values. They will dictate whether you think protest is an acceptable way of achieving those aims and your idea of what actions within protests are acceptable and unacceptable. Furthermore, your ethics also mean that you are likely to consider some causes more just than others. Protests cover a wide range of issues, some of which will seem worthy and some of which will seem offensive.

Consider the following exercise to help you start to understand your own ethical stance on protests and your beliefs about the acceptability of some of the causes.

Explore your thinking

• How do you feel about the following causes that have all been represented through protest?

Cause of protest	Strongly support	Mildly support	Indifferent	Mildly against	Strongly against
Animal rights					
Pro-fox hunting					
Black Lives Matter					
Anti-Brexit					
Pro-Brexit					
Extinction Rebellion					
HS2					
Just Stop Oil					
Anti-fracking					
Anti-nuclear					
Anti-capitalism					

Sometimes you may feel more or less sympathetic towards a cause that is being protested and this can also cause you to feel more or less sympathetic and connected to the people involved in that protest.

• What characteristics do you associate with the following types of protestors?

   – environmental activists;

   – anti-war protestors;

   – far right activists;

   – anti-abortion protestors;

   – Me Too movement.

It may be that when you were considering the types of protestors, you instinctively conjured up a stereotypical image of the type of person involved in those protests and the characteristics you associate with that type of person.

It is important to recognise this so you can understand your own emotions and what may be driving your decision making and the way you behave in a protest situation. You may stereotype different types of protests and protestors, associating more negative characteristics with some than others. This can impact on the way you engage and behave with the protestors. Remember that they are also likely to have assumptions and stereotypical views about the police so this can be a barrier to communication too and may make your job a little more difficult and frustrating.

By recognising this and understanding your emotions and feelings, it can help you to manage them. HMICFRS (2021b) make the point that protests exist because there is something that is controversial and there are conflicting viewpoints about the issue. Sometimes this can be distasteful to others and can represent a minority view. Nevertheless, you have a positive duty to safeguard the rights of the protestors when engaging in a peaceful protest. You need to be aware of any stereotypes that you may instinctively conjure up and manage your behaviours to ensure that you are challenging your own assumptions and policing fairly and impartially whatever the subject of the protest, and whoever is involved in the protest.

Use of powers

While the right to peaceful protest is enshrined under ECHR, it is a qualified right. Therefore, there are times where, as a police officer, you will be able to interfere with that right.

The first instance appears to be the most straightforward and that is when a protest is no longer peaceful. However, even the decision making around how to manage this is not as clear-cut as it may at first appear. At what stage should the police intervene when there are minor offences being committed? Should the police always intervene when serious violence or serious offences are being committed? How much force should the police use in these circumstances?

The second instance is when the protest is peaceful but is highly disruptive and new legislation has recently been introduced to help you manage these situations. In either case you need to know what legislation you are acting under and what powers are available to you. Once you know what you can do legally, then you also have to consider the proportionality and necessity of your actions. These issues are discussed in the following sections.

Knowledge of legislation

When making decisions while policing a protest you should be using the national decision model (NDM) to support your decision making. One step of that model is to consider your powers and policies. There is a range of legislation that is available to you to support you in the policing of protests. If you have had the benefit of a briefing prior to your deployment, then some of these powers may be outlined to you there.

Some of the key pieces of legislation which will support you in the policing of a protest are:

• Public Order Act 1986;

• Highways Act 1980;

• Offences Against the Person Act 1861;

• Criminal Damage Act 1971;

• Police, Crime, Sentencing and Courts Act 2022.

It is not possible in this book to discuss the specific legislation but for an in-depth discussion on this issue see the House of Commons briefing paper on police powers in protest (Brown and Mead, 2021).

Some protestors will have taken part in many more protests than you will have policed. Some are professional people; some have legal qualifications. Some will be fully armed with their rights and the legislation and nuances of case law. This can feel intimidating when you are faced with such individuals in a high-pressure situation. Sometimes they will be well informed; sometimes they may be misinformed.

Case law also helps to interpret the practical application of the legislation. For example, when does obstruction of a highway actually become an obstruction? To what extent does the highway need to be obstructed and for what period of time? etc. You can find case law through the BAILII website (www.bailii.org). As case law tends to be written in very formal and legal language, it can be difficult to fully absorb the points it makes. However, the Police National Legal Database should be able to assist you with a more practical description of the relevant points from case law that may impact on your policing practice.

There is no substitute for knowing the legislation and understanding it, so if you feel that you have gaps in your knowledge then revisit the legislation and speak to your training department or supervisor to help you clarify anything you are unsure about. The College of Policing Authorised Professional Practice site also provides further guidance that you should be familiar with to support you in exercising your powers properly when policing protests.

In the earlier scenario, legally you would have a power to act. However, you then need to consider the proportionality and necessity of any proposed action.

Proportionality and necessity

When considering proportionality and necessity, there are several things to consider.

• Is the objective important enough to justify acting, for example, removing protestors from a location, preventing damage, preventing violence etc?

- Will the intervention (your action) meet the objective, for example, will arresting someone stop the damage?
- Are the means used to achieve the objective no more than necessary or could a less intrusive method be used without compromising the objective, for example, do you need to arrest someone causing an obstruction or could you simply ask them to move or perhaps escort them away?
- On balance, does the action to meet the objective outweigh the severity of the effects on the person it is applied to, for example, does using force on protestors to prevent serious violence outweigh the potential harm that may be caused to the protestors?
(summarised from *Bank Mellat v HM Treasury*, 2013, paras 72–74)

This is the part of the national decision model where you will consider your options and you can use these principles to help you determine the most appropriate action. In essence, consider the reasonableness of your actions and, in common parlance, don't use a sledgehammer to crack a nut. This may seem quite obvious but the decision making around proportionality and necessity can be more nuanced. Consider the following example and your own thoughts about it and what action you might have taken.

Explore your thinking

You may remember the incident during protests in Bristol when the statue of Edward Colston was pulled down and thrown into the harbour. The statue was controversial because while Colston was a philanthropist and had provided a lot of money for the city, he had also profited from the slave trade during the seventeenth century. The media reported widely on this event and there were criticisms as the police did not intervene to prevent the statue being toppled and tipped into the harbour.

- What do you think about the police action in that situation?
- What reasons do you think the police had for not intervening?

This is a difficult situation and instinctively as a police officer you may think it is wrong to stand by and watch criminal damage happening. However, HMICFRS (2021b) reviewed this case and found criticisms of police inaction once the damage had started to be unwarranted. They provided the words of the Chief Constable of Avon and Somerset as a clear and sensible explanation:

the commanders on the ground made the decision that to intervene to arrest suspects would likely lead to injuries to suspects, injuries to officers. People who were not involved in damaging property being drawn into a very violent confrontation with the police that could have had serious ramifications for the city of Bristol and beyond.

Can you imagine scenes of police in Bristol fighting with protesters who were damaging the image, the statue, of a man, who is reputed to have gathered much of his fortune through the slave trade? I think there would have been very serious implications.

(HMICFRS, 2021b, p 70)

Questions that you would need to ask yourself here are what are the risks associated with acting compared to not acting? Is it possible to bring the offenders to justice at a later stage without compromising any public safety? The proportionality and the necessity of taking immediate action need to be weighed against the potential outcomes and likelihood of greater harm. These are not easy decisions to make but by having a clear rationale for your action, or lack of action, your decision making becomes transparent and defensible.

Discretion

When policing a protest, it is highly likely that there will be an overall commander and some planning will have taken place prior to your deployment. The commander will set the overall strategy for the operation and will often set the overall tone and style of the policing response too. It is important that you are aware of the tone and style that is expected so that you can tailor your actions and develop your decision making in line with the overall strategy.

Having said this, as a police officer you do have the power of discretion. This means that you are individually accountable for your own decision making. It allows you to draw on your experience, knowledge and assessment of the situation happening in front of you. It allows you to use your judgement to decide on the best course of action.

Having discretion doesn't mean that you can just do what you want though. You still need to be able to explain and justify your decisions. Sometimes whatever decision you make will draw criticism from one quarter or another. However, you are unlikely to get into trouble if you are able to coherently and logically explain your decision drawing on these principles.

Professionalism

As a police officer at a protest, you may be working long hours and be subject to constant recording and postings on social media. This can be a stressful and a difficult situation and lead you to questioning yourself about your own actions. There have been reports of commanders witnessing a reluctance to use powers:

a palpable nervousness to use power and force in protest situations by younger officers drawn from frontline and other non-specialist duties... Officers deployed in pressure situations and under intense real-time scrutiny through mobile devices, fear doing the wrong thing and getting into trouble.

(HMICFRS, 2021b, p 88)

This can lead to inaction and officers choosing to do nothing as it is easier rather than taking action where it is appropriate. If you decide to take no action, then this should be subject to the same level of decision making as actually choosing to do something. Inaction should be a justifiable, reasoned and defensible decision in its own right. As a professional police officer, you have to be able to take on the responsibility for making a decision to either take positive action or making a conscious decision to take no action and you have to be prepared to be able to explain that decision. Whatever decision you make, someone may be recording it so ensure you act with professionalism at all times.

Communication and conflict management

There will be occasions during the policing of protests where you need to use force. Again, you need to be able to justify each individual use of force considering the necessity and proportionality and weighing it against the risks posed. A study by HMICFRS (2021b) found that while there was widespread support for the use of force to stop violent protests, a majority of people surveyed thought it was unacceptable to use force against non-violent protests. Of course, public opinion does not drive policing decision making but you should be cognisant of it and the effect it can have on the broader concept of policing by consent.

This again presents a need for careful decision making when policing peaceful but highly disruptive protests and also when dealing with minor offences as there is a balance to meet with regard to the level of force you may use. This book is not intended to tell you when you should or should not use force and how much is acceptable as that is an operational decision based on the factors in front of you. However, protests are policed with an aim of engagement and open dialogue so it is worth a brief discussion about alternative options to try to prevent an escalation to the use of force and communication skills that may assist you.

Explore your thinking

When policing a protest, you may be subject to 'relentless insults and abuse' (HMICFRS, 2021b, p 41). Perhaps you have experienced this but if not then try to imagine this scenario.

• How did/would this make you feel?

• How did/would you respond to the constant insults?

• Do you think your response could impact on how the situation unfolds?

Any form of communication is a two-way process and the way that you choose to respond to insulting, disrespectful or unpleasant communication may either aggravate or calm any given situation.

The Betari Box is a model that may help you to understand how situations can escalate (see Figure 2.1).

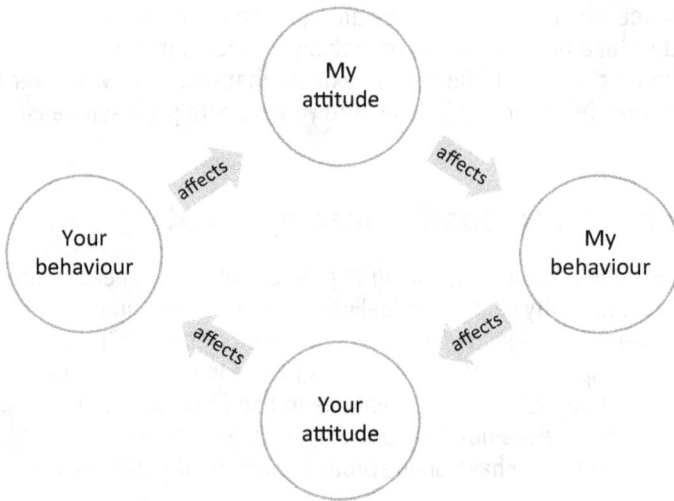

Figure 2.1 Betari Box

In essence, what this model is saying is that if you are faced with passive aggression or insulting behaviour and language it can put you in a certain mindset and mood, an attitude which can then lead you to behave according to your mood. For instance, if the protestors annoy or irritate you then you may be short and snappy or more authoritarian with them. This behaviour will then affect their attitude and the way they behave.

You are likely to be tired, working a long shift and your feelings may already be running high so it can be easy to see how this could escalate. Be aware of your own reactions to how they are making you feel. You are there as a professional and while it can be easy to be condescending, impolite, overly directive or authoritarian in response to the provocation, you need to work hard to maintain a neutral, polite but firm attitude. Of course, there may be times where you need to be more assertive but constructive dialogue aimed at diffusing a situation rather than enflaming it should be a key skill that you work to develop.

During the G20 protests in 2009, protestors were subjected to containment. One of the key criticisms was that the protestors did not know what was happening or why and this led to increased resentment and anxiety (Brown and Mead, 2021). Remember it is not only the decision that is made but the way it is conveyed that can make a difference. Therefore, do not be afraid to engage appropriately with protestors, explain calmly and clearly what is happening, and where appropriate try to answer their questions and engage in a dialogue, adapting your communication appropriately.

Key points

- Remember that there is a right to peaceful protest and you have a positive duty to protect those exercising this right.
- You should police in line with the overall tone of the operation set by the commander.
- You need to understand the legal powers available to you.
- You should act legally, proportionately, where necessary and with professionalism.
- Sometimes there is no right answer, just the better option for that moment.
- Make sure you can explain and justify your actions.

Further reading

An essential source of information to inform your practice is the College of Policing Authorised Professional Practice site on policing protests, which can be found at: www.college.police.uk/app/public-order/core-principles-and-legislation/core-principles-and-legislation

Circular 005/2022 updates the police on the introduction of the Police, Crime, Sentencing and Courts Act 2022 and it can be found at: www.gov.uk/government/publications/circular-0052022-police-crime-sentencing-and-courts-act-2022

Part 2

Managing risk and safeguarding: complex decision making

Chapter 3
Identifying and managing risk: stalking and harassment

Learning objectives

By the end of this chapter you should be able to:

- differentiate between harassment and stalking;

- identify behaviours that may be associated with stalking;

- explain why accurate risk assessment and management is crucial in stalking cases;

- understand your own perceptions of stalking victims and behaviours and how they can impact on your actions;

- explain how the information you gather during an investigation can be used by other agencies to help manage risk.

Introduction

This chapter examines the decisions you may be faced with when investigating harassment and stalking offences. Harassment and stalking form part of the government Violence Against Women and Girls strategy as offences that disproportionately affect women. It is reported that almost a quarter of women (23.3 per cent) have been subjected to stalking since the age of 16 (Office for National Statistics, 2022a). Research has also revealed that '*stalking is a key indicator for future potential serious harm*' (Monckton-Smith et al, 2004, p 3). Therefore, the decisions you make in these investigations, including the way that you identify and manage risk, are vital to safeguarding and protecting victims and supporting the criminal justice process.

This chapter explores the importance of properly identifying the offence initially as all your other actions will follow from this decision. It specifically examines the information-gathering phase of the national decision model and focuses on how risk is identified, assessed and managed by the police and how this links to decision making and actions. It asks readers to explore their own assumptions about harassment and stalking and how this can influence the way that they view risk and perceptions of victims and suspects. This chapter also explores how your actions and the information you gather is vital to support the decision making of others involved in the wider criminal justice process.

Scenario

Yesterday I attended a report by a woman that a man has assaulted her and tried to steal her phone. When I arrived, I was met by a young woman who was very upset and crying. She was being comforted by her boyfriend and family.

She said that she had been out for the evening. She had come home and a couple of her friends had returned shortly afterwards with the man who she works with. She had had previous problems with him so she was unhappy that he was there and they had an argument and she left. He followed her and was calling to her. She was on the phone to her boyfriend and he had grabbed at her hand and in the process had pulled some of her hair, causing pain but no injury. A passing car stopped and picked her up and took her to her boyfriend's house where the police then attended.

She said that she had previously reported some behaviour to the police last month. She said that the colleague had been loitering and waiting for her outside her house, her car had suffered some damage and he had also sent her some flowers. She said that she was friends with him outside of work and she thinks perhaps he has got the wrong idea. On that occasion, the police had phoned the man and gave him words of advice about his behaviour.

As we left, my colleague joked that they wished someone would send them flowers and that it seemed to be a case of a lovesick man making a clumsy attempt to woo her. My colleague said that it would be classified as harassment but was really low level and probably wouldn't go anywhere because it would be impossible to prove the man was responsible for a lot of what the victim had complained about. My colleague said the victim seemed to have an overactive imagination and seemed a bit neurotic.

Today we interviewed the man and during interview he admitted grabbing the phone, admitted waiting outside her home, admitted following her and admitted sending her flowers. However, he said they had been in an on-and-off relationship for some time and produced text messages to prove this, detailing contact between them over the preceding days.

My colleague seemed really annoyed that the woman had lied about the relationship and had wasted our time. My colleague said to me that the CPS would never prosecute in these circumstances and therefore they phoned the woman and told her that the police would not be taking any further action as there was insufficient evidence to support any complaint.

Explore your thinking

Having read the above scenario, think about these initial questions.

- Do you think the behaviours reported amounted to a lovesick would-be suitor, harassment or stalking?
- How much risk do you think the victim could be in?
- How did you feel when the prior relationship was revealed?
- How did it change your opinion of:
  - the victim;
  - the suspect;
  - the behaviours;
  - the risk?

Identifying harassment or stalking accurately, assessing and managing risk and conducting an effective investigation are key to protecting victims and achieving justice. However, these investigations present a number of difficulties. The behaviours are often low level and appear insignificant in themselves, so it can be easy to make assumptions, underestimate the risk and miss the investigative opportunities that these cases can present. By better understanding this area of offending, stalking behaviours and your reactions to victims, you can start to make more informed and defensible decisions.

History of harassment and stalking

In order to understand the decisions and actions you are expected to take in relation to these investigations, it can be helpful to explore how and why the legislation in this area developed. Knowing what legislation was intended to do can help with decision making around the application of it.

Introduction of harassment

Historically in England and Wales, the behaviours often associated with harassment and stalking were contained within a disparate set of legislation including the following:

- Malicious Communications Act 1988;
- Telecommunications Act 1984;
- Public Order Act 1986;

- Offences Against the Person Act 1861: threats to kill, ABH, and GBH;

- Criminal Justice and Public Order Act 1994: aggravated trespass;

- Criminal Justice Act 1988: common assault;

- Breach of the Peace.

Throughout the 1990s, there was an increasing public awareness of harassing and stalking behaviours (The Police Foundation, 2009). Calls for specific legislation to tackle these behaviours led the government to undertake a consultation to explore the extent of the problem and necessity for change.

In the subsequent House of Commons briefing report (Baber and Jeffs, 1996), it was recognised that there were gaps in the existing legislation. It did not cover all behaviours associated with harassment and stalking, some of which in themselves do not amount to criminal offences, and did not reflect the seriousness or the continuous nature of the offences. The report recommended new legislation to tackle these behaviours. As a result, the Protection from Harassment Act (PfHA) 1997 was enacted.

The PfHA 1997 introduced two offences of engaging in a course of conduct amounting to harassment: one causing alarm or distress (section 2) and the other putting a person in fear of violence (section 4). It also made provision for restraining orders on conviction or acquittal. The Act was always intended to deal with stalking behaviour but this was never defined or specifically mentioned within the legislation.

Introduction of stalking offences

Despite the introduction of the PfHA 1997, concerns remained over how the police were using the legislation. An independent parliamentary review reported that because the existing legislation did not specifically name stalking, these behaviours were becoming lost among nuisance offences and minor disputes (Llwyd, 2012).

Furthermore, it found that 72 per cent of victims surveyed for the report said they were unhappy with the criminal justice response. It identified that very few prosecutions under the existing legislation resulted in custodial sentences. Training around stalking behaviours for criminal justice practitioners was inadequate and there was a poor understanding of stalking behaviour by the police. In addition to this, risk assessments were not routinely being carried out.

As a result of these concerns, the Protection of Freedoms Act 2012 amended the PfHA 1997, creating two new additional offences of stalking. The first under section 2A creates an offence of stalking if it amounts to harassment (causing alarm or distress) and the acts or omissions are ones associated with stalking. The second offence under section 4A creates an offence of stalking that causes a fear of violence or serious alarm or distress. The amendment also introduced a new power of search under warrant in relation to stalking offences.

More recently, it has been recognised that early intervention to protect victims is necessary. Therefore, the Stalking Protection Act 2019 introduced a new civil Stalking Protection Order that allows the police to apply for an order to try to help to protect the victim at an early stage while an investigation is ongoing.

The evolution of the legislation and powers associated with it are in response to the recognition of the pervasive and serious nature of this type of offending. It recognises the risks that such behaviour can present and creates a legislative pathway to safeguarding victims and bringing offenders to justice.

The problems with harassment and stalking investigations

Despite the introduction of legislation to tackle this type of offending, there are still problems with the police response to harassment and stalking.

The scenario at the start of this chapter is based on a report made by 19-year-old Shana Grice in 2016 against Michael Lane (see IOPC, 2018 for full details). The victim account and the suspect account in the scenario are the broad circumstances that faced the investigating officer. As a result of the revelation of the relationship, the investigating officer discontinued the investigation. Shana was subsequently fined for wasting police time. No risk assessment was completed as the investigating officer determined the case was based on lies.

About four months later, Shana reported that Michael Lane had stolen her key and let himself into her bedroom while she slept. He was interviewed for 12 minutes and admitted the offence, but the interview was not placed in the context of the wider behaviour. He was cautioned for theft of a key and given a warning to cease contact with Shana.

Shana contacted the police another three times over the following month to report repeated stalking behaviours by him. No action was taken in relation to these reports. A few weeks later, Michael Lane broke into her house and murdered her.

A more recent case is the murder of Christie Frewin, who had also reported harassment, stalking and assault within a history of domestic assault by the offender Alex Staines. In that case the police were found to have failed to safeguard Christie and also failed to demonstrate professional curiosity and follow-up on lines of inquiry. The IOPC also found that the investigating officers *'appeared to take Mr Staines' account of events at face value, where Ms Frewin's account was repeatedly challenged and interrogated'* (IOPC, 2022b, para 17).

Sadly, these are not isolated incidents and highlight why making the right decisions and recognising and managing risk is so important.

An HMIC (2017) review into harassment and stalking identified a number of issues including:

• not recording the appropriate offence;

• not using available powers;

- risk assessments not done or done inadequately;

- risk management plans scarce;

- not identifying vulnerability;

- not taking victim personal statements;

- busy staff prematurely closing investigations.

In November 2022, the Suzy Lamplugh Trust submitted a super complaint against the police about the way that stalking offences were being handled. They identified that only 5 per cent of offences reported to police in the 12 months up to March 2022 resulted in a charge. The main issues they identified included the following.

- **Misidentification of stalking**
  - Lack of knowledge of the behaviours that constitute stalking.
  - Lack of knowledge of how stalking impacts on a victim.
  - Treating stalking reports as one-off incidents rather than in the pattern of behaviour.
  - Treating reports as low level, or minimising and trivialising reports.
- **Where stalking is identified, police not investigating appropriately**
  - Not gathering online evidence.
  - Not recognising links to homicide.
  - Failing to gather evidence for summary offences within six months and therefore leading to loss of the case.
  - Closing files without consultation with the Crown Prosecution Service (CPS), believing there was insufficient evidence.
- **Insufficient use of Stalking Protection Orders (SPOs)**
  - Not applying for SPOs.
  - Not responding to breach of SPOs in a timely manner.
  - Failing to deal with breaches of SPOs or other orders as new stalking offences.
  - Lack of referral to specialist services.

Identifying the offence

One of the key decisions you will make in an investigation such as this is what offence you record it as. Correct identification and recording of harassment or stalking are important because every other decision follows from this initial classification. The national decision model (NDM) starts with gathering information and intelligence. Listening to what the victim is telling you and asking questions to gather relevant information are crucial to you making an informed decision about the nature of the offence. You need to consider two things initially:

1. are there behaviours that amount to harassment?
2. is there a course of conduct?

Understanding the behaviours

A key problem with harassment and stalking is that the behaviours are often low level and therefore aren't always recognised as harassment. Harassment is not specifically defined but the CPS (2018, para 5) note that '*it can include repeated attempts to impose unwanted communications and contact upon a victim in a manner that could be expected to cause distress or fear in any reasonable person*'.

Remember that the PfHA 1997 was introduced because it was recognised that behaviours were not always criminal in themselves. Therefore, you should obtain a full history from the victim and note all the incidents, whether they appear insignificant individually or not, as that helps to establish a fuller picture about the overall offence.

There are a number of stalking myths that can affect the way you view the behaviours, including thinking that it is romantic or that the victim:

- is hysterical;
- is over-reacting;
- is imagining it;
- must have encouraged it;
- secretly likes it.

(McKeon et al, 2015)

This can be incredibly harmful and subjective assumptions such as these have no place within an investigative process.

The PfHA 1997 specifies that the suspect '*knows or ought to know*' that their behaviour amounts to harassment or that it would cause a fear of violence etc. The CPS (2018) offer the following advice:

> In determining whether the defendant ought to know that the course of his or her conduct will cause the other person to fear that violence will be used against them or will cause the other person serious alarm or distress, the question to be determined is whether a reasonable person in possession of the same information would think it so.

Therefore, you should not make any early assumptions based on your own beliefs and feelings. Instead, you should seek to explore the victim's account and gather evidence to demonstrate the nature and impact of the behaviour so that an informed decision can be made based on relevant information. This should also be a key line of questioning in any suspect interview. As the CPS (2018) point out, *'Ultimately, the decision as to what amounts to reasonable behaviour will rest with the courts'*.

Even if you feel on first account that you may struggle to prove some incidents, you should not dismiss them offhand. You should record them and consider, as part of a wider investigation plan, whether there are any further investigative actions you may be able to take to help corroborate the account.

You should also look for whether there is any apparent escalation in behaviours. Has there been a pattern of telephone calls and now the offender is loitering? Has loitering escalated to entering the victim's property etc? These are potentially significant risk factors and you should be exploring any escalation as you gather information about what has been happening.

Identifying a course of conduct

One of the main problems with identifying harassment and stalking is that incidents tend to be treated individually rather than being seen as a course of conduct. This can therefore lead to them being classified as other offences rather than harassment or stalking.

A course of conduct simply means an incident has occurred on at least two occasions. The behaviours do not have to be of the same nature; for example, there could have been one occasion of loitering outside a person's home and another of sending an unwanted gift. Of course, the more incidents, the stronger the evidence to demonstrate a course of conduct. One survey suggests that 70 per cent of victims suffer over 100 individual incidents before reporting matters to the police (Sheridan, 2005, cited in HMIC, 2017) so take the time to obtain the full history.

Differentiating between harassment and stalking

Once you have established that there is behaviour that amounts to harassment and there is a course of conduct, then you need to consider whether the offence is actually a higher-level offence of stalking. The PfHA 1997 states that stalking is harassment that exhibits stalking behaviours. It provides some examples of such behaviours including:

(a) *following a person,*

(b) *contacting, or attempting to contact, a person by any means,*

(c) *publishing any statement or other material relating or purporting to relate to a person, or purporting to originate from a person,*

(d) *monitoring the use by a person of the internet, email or any other form of electronic communication,*

(e) *loitering in any place (whether public or private),*

(f)   interfering with any property in the possession of a person,

(g)   watching or spying on a person.

To help you identify the difference between stalking and harassment, the mnemonic FOUR can be helpful as the behaviour will be **F**ixated, **O**bsessive, **U**nwanted and **R**epeated. Dictionary definitions of these words can help to give an understanding as to what this means:

- Fixated: *interested in someone or something to an excessive extent.*
- Obsessive: *thinking continually about someone or something.*
- Unwanted: *not wanted.*
- Repeated: *do again or more than once.*

(Oxford Dictionaries, 2013)

HMIC (2017) suggest that stalking is not being recognised and recorded appropriately. If the behaviours amount to harassment and appear to have the elements of FOUR then it should be treated as stalking.

Identifying opportunities for gathering supporting evidence

One of the criticisms of the policing of stalking is that the police are not always gathering evidence that could help to support a prosecution. Information forms the foundation of your decision making so you should develop an investigative plan *'pursuing all reasonable lines of inquiry, whether these lead towards or away from the suspect'* (Criminal Procedure and Investigations Act 1996). This includes exploring opportunities for corroborating the victim's account.

Explore your thinking

A victim has reported a number of stalking incidents and during her statement she tells you that yesterday she walked to her local supermarket. She saw the man who has been stalking her following behind. He followed her into the supermarket and stood at the end of every aisle watching her. While she was in the supermarket, she met one of her friends, who then stayed with her and walked her back home.

- What investigative opportunities may exist to corroborate the victim's account here?

- How might this support the decision making about charging or no further action?

You may have identified possible CCTV opportunities and also evidence from her friend. Evidence which has been corroborated is considered more reliable and can better support informed decision making.

Offenders may sometimes target the family and friends of their victims as well. This can form part of the harassment and stalking and therefore should not be ignored but should be treated as part of the incident. Evidence from other parties should therefore also be gathered to develop as full a picture as possible.

A particular issue with these types of offences is when they involve an element of online harassment or stalking. This has increased significantly and is a feature in many of these cases now. Research indicates that cyberstalking presents an unfamiliar challenge, creating professional uncertainty for the police who can feel ill-equipped to investigate due to the complexity and technological challenges involved (Martellozzo et al, 2022). This can lead to no attempts even being made to gather this evidence as sometimes there can be a presumption that it will be too difficult, too time-consuming and the police will not be able to attribute messages to the suspect. You should seek specialist advice before making any decisions about what evidence you may be able to recover where harassment or stalking behaviour involves an online element.

A key power that you need to consider is the specific power of entry, search and seizure under warrant for stalking offences. This can be used as an investigative tool to help you gather evidence where appropriate. Therefore, gathering information initially to identify what items may be relevant and could potentially be recovered during a search is crucial.

Establishing *'substantial adverse effect on the day-to-day activities of the victim'*

One element of the section 4A offence of stalking occurs when a person is caused serious alarm or distress that has a substantial adverse effect on the day-to-day activities of the victim.

Explore your thinking

Sandra used to be friends with a neighbour but after he asked her out and she declined he has been causing her problems. He repeatedly sends her unwanted messages on her social media, commenting on every post and tagging her into everything he does. He also posts false information about her sometimes. She has seen him standing in his garden staring at her house and he keeps showing up every time she goes out for an evening.

Sandra has stopped going out locally with her friends and has cancelled her social media accounts. She keeps her curtains closed, even during the day, as she feels uncomfortable and she avoids going into her garden. She has also contacted an estate agent and is trying to sell her house.

- How serious do you think the behaviours are?

- Do you think Sandra's reaction is proportionate to the behaviours?

- Do you think Sandra is suffering psychological harm as a result of the neighbour's behaviour?

- Do you think that the behaviours are causing a substantial adverse effect on her day-to-day activities?

You should not prejudge or minimise the effect but listen to the victim and gather their account. It may seem trivial and you may think that you would not be bothered by some behaviours. However, it is the relentless nature of these incidents that causes harm. Something that may appear trivial in isolation can have a real impact on physical and mental well-being.

Research shows that these behaviours can impact on every aspect of a victim's life, taking a physical, emotional and psychological toll (Taylor-Dunn et al, 2017). When the stalking behaviour is online it has been described as *'having a stalker in your pocket'* (Suzy Lamplugh Trust, 2022, p 21). Think about how often you check your own phone and imagine if you kept receiving messages that upset you but you never knew when you would get them. The cumulative effect of the behaviour causes the damage.

When you are gathering information, you need to explore the impact that the behaviours have had to help demonstrate a substantial adverse effect on daily activities. This could include changing phone number, changing job, stopping socialising, changing the place where they shop, moving home, changing daily routines, avoiding going to certain places, and so on (see Home Office, 2012 for further examples). This isn't about your opinion as to how you think the victim should have reacted to the behaviours but rather it is about the effect it actually had on the victim.

You should consider taking a victim personal statement at an early stage to evidence the impact the behaviour has had. This is not always done and the impact of the behaviours is not always gathered and presented by police. But it can help the decision makers at the CPS ensure the correct charge is laid if appropriate and, importantly, should the case progress to court it supports the imposition of the correct sentence reflecting the seriousness of the offence.

Identifying and managing the risk

Once you have gathered the information to allow you to establish the offence you are investigating, you then need to use that information to help assess and manage the risk.

Explore your thinking

Evidence suggests that risk assessments are not always completed.

• Why do you think this is?

• Could it be because officers are too busy?

• Is it that officers don't know what tool to use?

• Is it that officers don't see the value in risk assessments?

• What is your own view of risk assessments?

Remember that assessing threat and risk is a key part of the NDM and this is also the priority for your investigation. There are links between stalking and homicide, and these should not be underestimated. The risk may not be immediately obvious due to the low-level behaviours often reported but remember it is not the severity of the actions but the frequency, persistence and escalation that are important.

Risk assessment

Of course, not every report will end in homicide, but it can be difficult for you as an individual officer to accurately be able to predict risk just based on your own knowledge and experience.

Explore your thinking

• Does stranger stalking or ex-partner stalking present a higher risk?

• Does male offender/female victim present a higher risk than female offender/male victim?

Research has indicated that there is a common misconception that stranger stalkers pose more of a risk than acquaintance or ex-partner (Scott and Sheridan, 2011). However, the risks and violence associated with ex-partner stalking are actually higher. Correctly conducting a risk assessment utilising an appropriate recognised tool will help you identify this, but it is important that you don't make assumptions on the level of risk based on what you think you know.

Similarly, research has indicated that while female offender/male victim stalking is less frequent, there is no significant statistical difference in the use of violence (Strand and McEwan, 2012). Therefore, male victims should not be dismissed or their experiences lessened.

Your organisation will use risk assessment tools that are underpinned by research that you should use in every case to help you determine risk. However, initial risk assessments are sometimes not completed at all or are not fully completed answering all relevant questions. This means that risk is not properly identified and may leave the victim at risk of harm.

The risk assessment is a key part of your initial information-gathering phase and you need to spend the time to do this and understand the value of these tools. You should familiarise yourself with the risk management tools that your force uses and the policies around when and how they should be used and reviewed.

It is also important to understand that risk is not static. It can change over time and there-fore the risk assessment should be dynamic. If further incidents are reported, then the risk should be reassessed, particularly if there is an escalation in behaviour. Once the risk has been assessed then it also needs to be managed.

Risk management

HMIC (2017) found that in 61 per cent of the cases they examined there was no risk man-agement plan. A risk management plan should look at mitigating or removing risk wherever possible. However, you need to be mindful about how you achieve this.

Explore your thinking

Imagine you went to a pub in your local town centre. While you were there, a fight started and you were assaulted. You reported it to the police and they told you to stop going to the pub and to keep away from the town centre altogether.

• How would that make you feel?

It is likely that you would feel aggrieved that you had been the victim of a crime but you were being asked to change your behaviours and stop your normal activities.

Now think about a victim who has reported receiving unwanted phone calls from a man and he waits and watches her when she collects her children from school. She has been advised to change her phone number and arrange for someone else to collect her children from school.

• How do you think the victim might perceive this advice?

While on the face of it such advice might seem logical and protective, it can actually alienate the victim, making them feel like they are to blame. The advice can feel punitive to the victim who is being asked to change their behaviours and can worsen the impact of the harassment or stalking. Such advice can increase isolation, for example by stopping the victim interacting on social media, seeing people they usually meet and preventing their routine activities.

Similarly, you should not encourage the victim to undertake behaviours just so that you can gather more evidence, such as advising them to confront the suspect if they see them loitering or recording the suspect if they phone. Such behaviours could actually increase risk. Instead, you should offer appropriate safety advice to the victim and consider referral to a support service. The Suzy Lamplugh Trust offers advocacy services and also has a variety of safety guides that may be useful for victims to support them (see: www.suzylamplugh. org/Pages/Category/personal-safety-advice).

The Home Office (2021, p 32) emphasise that investigators should not judge victims who do not appear to follow safety advice and should not label them as uncooperative, but instead recognise that levels of resilience and individual circumstances vary.

A key development in tackling stalking has been the introduction of Stalking Protection Orders (SPOs). These should form part of your risk management plan and need early consideration in stalking cases. The threshold to commence criminal proceedings is not necessary for an order. Their purpose is to try to protect the victim and stop the stalking behaviours as an early intervention. They are not a replacement for a criminal investigation but a tool to allow you to protect the victim whie you conduct an investigation. There is comprehensive guidance for the police that you should familiarise yourself with about applying for these orders (Home Office, 2021). Liaison with the victim and understanding their views around risks are vital to this process as you can apply for prohibitions or requirements on the person subject to the order based on the risk assessment and information gathered.

By its nature, harassment and stalking are ongoing so the longer your investigation takes the more opportunity the offender has to continue or escalate their behaviours. Therefore, early intervention and effective investigation are key to managing risk.

The PfHA 1997 also provides a power to apply for a restraining order whether a person is convicted or acquitted. When applying for an order, the victim's views should be taken into account and this can be granted when the judge considers it is necessary to prevent harm and is proportionate to the threat. These orders are preventative not punitive and are aimed at protecting people from stalking behaviours.

A prompt investigation, utilising early intervention tools and responding quickly and effectively to breaches of any SPOs or restraining orders is vital to help safeguard the victim.

Understanding how your investigation is used by others to inform decision making

When investigators conduct an investigation, it is like a mosaic that is pieced together (Innes et al, 2021). In order to understand the information that is coming in, investigators indulge in a sense-making process where they add meaning and weight to different pieces of information. When you then present an investigation, it is a narrative that you have created that interprets and draws attention to key issues that you have deemed important. The narrative that you create and the way you interpret and present the information can impact on the mindset of your supervisors when making a decision about further action.

In the Shana Grice case, the investigating officer briefed his supervisor, emphasising the lie rather than the admissions made by the suspect. In that case the detective inspector said he was aware of previous incidents but *'he did not research the incidents, and would not routinely do so as he relies on the officer in the case to provide him with relevant information'* (IOPC, 2018, para 206).

The CPS will work with the material that you have provided in order to determine the most appropriate charge where relevant. Therefore, the risk assessment and victim personal statement should form part of the case file at this stage, along with the investigative material you have gathered, to enable CPS to make an informed and justified decision. The NPCC and CPS (2018) protocol provides valuable information for you about how the police and CPS should work together on these cases.

Prisons and probation also need accurate information to assess appropriate rehabilitation or treatment programmes and any conditions that may be applied. Also, processes such as MARAC or MAPPA will draw on investigative material that you have recovered. Perhaps you can appreciate how important your individual investigation and your decision making within that investigation are when dealing with these offences.

Key points

- You need to spend time on the gathering information section of the NDM to properly understand what you are investigating, and the risks associated with it.

- Risk assessment and management should be at the forefront of the investigation.

- Harassment and stalking offences often involve low-level incidents but need to be seen within the context of a course of conduct.

- Your initial decision making about classifying an offence can have implications for decision making throughout the criminal justice system.

- Be aware of how your assumptions about offender behaviours and victim reactions can impact on your mindset and decision making.

Further reading

The College of Policing Authorised Professional Practice site is essential reading for you and provides advice for first attending officers and also investigators, as well as information about Stalking Protection Orders. It can be accessed at: www.college.police.uk/app/major-investigation-and-public-protection/stalking-or-harassment

Chapter 4
Prosecuting or safeguarding: juveniles involved in criminality

Learning objectives

By the end of this chapter you should be able to:

- explain why children involved in county lines drug dealing are in the first instance to be considered victims of trafficking and/or exploitation;

- understand that county lines is a form of abuse that seeks to exploit and coerce children and vulnerable people to become involved in criminal activity;

- understand the role you play as a police officer to protect and safeguard children involved in county lines;

- explain the National Referral Mechanism (NRM) and the referral process;

- identify the signs when a child or young person may be involved in criminal exploitation.

Introduction

This chapter explores the operational challenges faced by frontline officers dealing with children and vulnerable people who have been trafficked and/or exploited into county lines drug dealing. The Home Office (2018, p 2) define county lines as 'a term used to describe gangs and organised criminal networks involved in exporting illegal drugs into one or more areas within the UK, using dedicated mobile phone lines or other form of "deal line" '. They are likely to exploit children and vulnerable adults to move and store the drugs and money and they will often use coercion, intimidation, violence (including sexual violence) and weapons (College of Policing, 2021).

This chapter explores how the criminal justice system responds to occasions when a child or young person is identified as a potential victim of county lines exploitation. It will also examine the frustrations and experiences of police officers who feel the system has tipped too far in favour of the child, resulting in some avoiding prosecution even when involved in serious violent crime, Class A drug dealing or repeat offending.

The chapter uses a fictional scenario to explore your thinking. You are encouraged to consider how you approach young people involved in county lines drug supply and how your operational experience of county lines influences your decision making.

Finally, the chapter discusses the importance of safeguarding and how to recognise a child or young person as a potentially exploited victim, and how using the national decision model (NDM) will enable you to structure your reasoning in a way that ensures that NRM decision makers have available to them all the required information to come to an informed decision when making a conclusive grounds decision on whether that child or vulnerable person is a victim of modern slavery.

Scenario

While on mobile patrol in a high-crime area well known for Class A street dealing, you see a young person exit a car. They see your marked vehicle and run away. You PNC the vehicle; it is registered to an address 70 miles away and there is a marker indicating that the vehicle is involved in county lines drug dealing. Before you can stop the vehicle, it drives away.

30 minutes later you see the same young person but this time they are speaking to someone who is known to you as a heroin user. You observe an exchange. You stop and speak to the young person that you'd seen earlier. You become aware that a phone in their possession is continually ringing. Based on what you know and have observed, you are considering your Section 23 Misuse of Drugs Act 1971 search powers, but your colleague is somewhat dismissive having experienced similar scenarios. They share with you their point of view that the young person will never be charged if drugs are found as they will claim they're being exploited and you will spend the rest of the shift completing paperwork.

You continue to question the young person but they are unwilling to explain why they are there or what they are doing. They provide their name and date of birth; they are 15 years-old and live in the same town that the vehicle he exited is registered at. They become confrontational and aggressive towards you when you ask how they came to have an injury to their face. Their behaviour suddenly changes and they begin to cry. They continually say that they 'haven't done nothing wrong' and question why you have stopped them.

Given what you had observed and the information known, you are satisfied that the grounds for reasonable suspicion are met and you proceeded to conduct a Section 23 Misuse of Drugs Act 1971 search. Although no drugs are found, they are in possession of two phones: one appears to be a 'burner' phone, the other their personal phone. You ask your colleague whether you should seize the phones as possible evidence of drugs supply. Your colleague says it would be easier if you had a quick look at the messages on the device to see if any related to drug supply. If there wasn't you could let the young person go on their way and there would be no paperwork to complete.

Explore your thinking

Think about how you would have reacted to this situation. Consider the following questions.

- Would you have considered the young person to be a victim of criminal exploitation?
  - If yes, what victim indicators are present that might suggest they are involved in county lines?
  - If no, what is your reasoning for coming to this decision?
- Why do you think the young person appeared confrontational and aggressive?
- Would you have examined the mobile phone at the time of the search in an attempt to locate messages which may indicate their involvement in drug supply?
  - If yes, what police powers would you have used to seize and examine the device there and then?
  - If no, would you consider seizing the mobile phone for examination at the police station. If so, what grounds and police powers would you use?
  - If your decision is not to seize, retain and review the content of the mobile phone, explain your reasoning.
- Although no drugs were found, do you think that there was sufficient suspicion to suspect their involvement in the supply of drugs and arrest?
  - If yes, what are your reasonable grounds for believing that the young person's arrest is necessary?
  - If no, given the circumstances, what steps would you consider to safeguard and protect the young person?

Background: what is county lines?

County lines drug dealing is a term used to describe organised crime groups (OCGs) who supply drugs outside of larger urban areas into suburban areas, including market and coastal towns. Offending through county lines is a national issue involving the exploitation of thousands of vulnerable children and adults by violent gang members in order to move and sell crack cocaine and heroin.

At its simplest level, county lines involves moving drugs from one part of the country to another and when there is use of dedicated mobile phone lines to take orders and supply drugs. Once in these smaller communities, drug dealers often target vulnerable people and take over their homes, a practice commonly referred to as 'cuckooing'. The home is used to facilitate local drug supply, including storing, weighing and packaging of drugs, and to store weapons.

In recent years these small towns and communities, which were previously unaffected by the serious violence associated with drug supply at street level, have experienced a significant increase in gun and knife crime. In 2020, the National Crime Agency (NCA) said that exploitation in county lines drug dealing was *'the most frequently identified form of coerced criminality, with children representing the vast majority of victims'* (NCA, 2020, p 24). In 2021, at least 14.5 per cent of modern slavery referrals were related to county lines activity (Havard, 2022).

This type of drugs supply operation presents law enforcement with a number of challenges, particularly as those involved rarely see themselves as trafficked or exploited victims of crime. In the UK in 2020, approximately 40 per cent of all child referrals to the National Referral Mechanism (NRM) for criminal exploitation were identified as being involved in county lines (Caluori, 2021). According to the NCA, the average age of children involved in county lines drug dealing is 15.8 years, although there have been reports of children as young as 12 years-old being involved in county lines (Home Office, 2018).

The exploitation of children and vulnerable people by older, more violent, gang members is central to the success of county lines and without their exploitation it couldn't exist as a criminal business model (HM Government, 2016).

County lines and children: understanding the law

The Modern Slavery Act 2015 provides a statutory defence for victims of child trafficking and exploitation accused of certain offences for those who are compelled to commit criminal offences.

Where a child commits an offence and they do so as a direct consequence of being or having been a victim of modern slavery or trafficking, section 45 of the Modern Slavery Act 2015 provides a defence. It states that a child will not be guilty of an offence if:

(a) *the person is under 18 when the person does the act which constitutes the offence,*

(b) *the person does that act as a direct consequence of the person being, or having been, a victim of slavery or a victim of relevant exploitation, and*

(c) *a reasonable person in the same situation as the person and having the person's 'relevant characteristics' would have no realistic alternative to committing the act.*

Relevant characteristics means age, sex, and any physical or mental illness or disability.

The criminal exploitation of a child or young person will almost certainly involve a wide range of criminal activity associated with county lines, which means that police and CPS prosecutors, on a case-by-case basis, can consider different legislation which fully reflects their involvement so that the correct criminal justice outcome can be achieved. The type of offences will range considerably but typically these include:

- drugs-related offences;
- assault, including sexual assault;
- gun and knife crime;
- robbery;
- kidnap and blackmail offences;
- theft.

Being able to recognise the related offences at an early stage of the investigation will ensure that you have the necessary information to manage any potential and immediate risks and take appropriate safeguarding action. When a child comes to your notice as a part of your safeguarding actions, you will refer to the local authority children's services and to the NRM.

In this scenario, the officer sought to seize and retain the mobile phone to conduct an examination to establish whether the device contained incriminating messages of drug supply.

Under section 23 of the Misuse of Drugs Act 1971, if a police officer has reasonable grounds to suspect a person is in possession of a controlled drug they may seize anything found in the course of the search which appears to be evidence of an offence under the Act; that includes a mobile phone.

The mobile phone may be seized for the purposes of criminal investigation and retained so long as it necessary in all the circumstances. In this case it was seized for forensic digital examination (PACE 1984, s 22). Police officers and investigators need to be aware of their force policy to avoid the suggestion that an unauthorised or inappropriate search affected the forensic integrity of the device so as to render any evidence gathered inadmissible.

National Referral Mechanism

The National Referral Mechanism (NRM) is a framework for identifying and referring potential victims of modern slavery and ensuring they receive the appropriate support and to establish their trafficking status. If the potential victim is under 18, or may be under 18, an NRM referral must be made. Child victims do not have to consent to be referred to the NRM. Before a referral is made, the investigator will need to ensure that all immediate safeguarding and welfare needs of the child have been met (Home Office, 2023).

The total number of potential child victims referred into the NRM process from 1 July to 30 September 2022 was 4586, of which 577 referrals were flagged as county lines referrals, accounting for 13 per cent of all referrals received. The majority, 76 per cent (437), of these referrals were male children (Home Office, 2022b).

Investigating and prosecuting those responsible for coercing or exploiting a child for a modern slavery offence can be complex and challenging. Crown Prosecution Service (CPS) guidance encourages prosecutors to consider prosecuting those organising and facilitating county lines cases under the Modern Slavery Act *'in circumstances where there has been deliberate targeting, recruitment and significant exploitation of young and vulnerable people'*. However, it also says prosecutors should be *'alert to the challenge of securing a conviction for a Modern Slavery Act offence'* (CPS, 2022a).

We explore later in this chapter the investigative approach you will need to consider when gathering evidence to support a modern slavery offence within a county lines prosecution.

Explore your thinking

Take a few minutes to think about a child or young person and the journey they will likely have taken to be at a point where they find themselves in an unfamiliar town selling Class A drugs on behalf of violent older gang members to people they don't know.

• Note down the signs to look out for which indicate a child may be involved in county lines activity.

You may have noted common indicators such as unexplained acquisition of money, clothes or mobile phones, significant decline in school attendance or parental concerns. Early identification of a child at risk of county lines exploitation with the appropriate safeguarding referrals may provide an opportunity to protect the child and divert them away from this type of harm.

Other signs to look out for include the following.

• *Persistently going missing from school or home and/or being found out of the area.*

• *Excessive receipt of texts/phone calls or having multiple handsets.*

• *Relationships with controlling/older individuals or groups.*

• *Leaving home/care without explanation.*

• *Suspicion of physical assault or unexplained injuries.*

• *Carrying weapons.*

• *Gang association or isolation from friends or social networks.*

• *Unwillingness to explain their whereabouts.*

• *Travelling to locations or being found in areas with which they have no obvious connection.*

• *Being isolated from peers or social networks.*

(Home Office, 2018)

Explore your thinking

When a child has been identified as a potential victim, they need to be appropriately protected and safeguarded. Take a few minutes to think about the reporting processes in your police force.

• Note down what reporting mechanism and processes are in place when a child comes to your notice through their involvement in county lines.

• Think about what information and support services are available in your force area for parents or those with parental responsibility who have concerns and for the young person involved, together with where you can readily access this information.

Where you have assessed that a child or young person has been harmed or is at risk of harm, every effort should be made to safeguard and protect that child or young person. To do this you must be familiar with your relevant force policies and procedures and know what police powers are available to you.

Contemporary issues

Appropriate use of statutory defence section 45 of the Modern Slavery Act 2015 and the National Referral Mechanism

Some police officers are concerned that this statutory defence is used as an opportunity to avoid a criminal justice outcome. This point was highlighted in a 'call for evidence' by the Independent Anti-Slavery Commissioner when evidence from the police colloquially referred to the statutory defence as the 'county lines defence' with officers not associating the defence with modern slavery, but with drug dealing (Independent Anti-Slavery Commissioner, 2020).

Police officers frequently report instances where children and young people are arrested, often on multiple occasions, on suspicion of being involved in serious crime including blackmail, Class A drug dealing, possession of knives and serious assault, who then raise section 45 as their defence. These concerns were acknowledged in 2019 when an independent review of the Modern Slavery Act was undertaken.

The final report read:

> The Act provides a statutory defence for victims of modern slavery for certain criminal offences that they were compelled to carry out as a result of their exploitation. The review looked at how to ensure an appropriate balance between the need to protect victims from criminal prosecution and preventing criminals from abusing this protection

to avoid justice. The resulting challenges and that disproving a claim of exploitation or trafficking beyond reasonable doubt could be challenging.

(Field et al, 2019, p 18)

The review concluded that existing legislation and criminal justice process achieved the right balance and made a recommendation that *'law enforcement and prosecutors should conduct thorough investigations to gather sufficient evidence to demonstrate whether an individual using the statutory defence is a victim'* (p 18).

Interestingly, the Magistrates Association also recognised concerns with the way in which section 45 was approached and in particular that some young people who had been criminally exploited were reluctant to use this defence as a means to help their case because of a fear of being labelled a 'grass' (Gammon and Easton, 2019).

The NRM is a framework designed to enable the police and other first responders to identify victims of modern slavery and refer them on to the appropriate support services. Although the NRM is a civil process where decisions are made on the balance of probabilities, it often comes into conflict with the criminal justice system as the CPS will pause court proceedings until a conclusive grounds decision has been reached on whether the individual is a victim of modern slavery or not.

However, just because an individual has received a positive decision from the NRM that they are a victim of modern slavery, that doesn't mean that a prosecution will always cease. The CPS position is that *'a case should not be dropped simply because the suspect or defendant had claimed they were the victim of modern slavery as these decisions are based on a balance of probabilities'* (CPS, 2022a).

There are also occasions where a section 45 defence is raised at or immediately prior to trial, leaving the prosecution little or no time to consider what evidence is available to support or rebut the defence. At this point, it is important to remember that the burden of proof falls upon the police and prosecution to disprove the defence beyond reasonable doubt. Therefore, police officers and investigators need to be alert to the possibility that this defence may be raised at any point during proceedings and ensure that their investigation plan has, from the outset, had this defence at the forefront of their mind.

Explore your thinking

As a police officer, a key part of your role is to keep individuals and the public safe and to detect crime. However, in county lines cases there appears to be a reluctance among police officers to identify suspects as potential victims of trafficking because of the mistaken belief that it automatically would prevent any prosecution if they raise section 45 as a defence (Independent Anti-Slavery Commissioner, 2020).

You may have experienced a suspect who said that they were exploited or forced into selling drugs, or involved in other linked criminality, but their previous history of arrests and involvement in criminality caused you to question whether they were trying to use a section 45 defence as a 'loophole' to avoid prosecution.

• How did it make you feel when the decision was made not to proceed with a prosecution?

Take a few minutes to think about a particular case and ask yourself the following question: Did the police conduct a thorough investigation looking towards and away from the suspect's involvement to provide enough evidence for the CPS to properly test each limb of the statutory section 45 defence?

• What could you have done differently in your case presentation to the CPS for a charging decision?

• What other evidential opportunities were there which you could have secured and presented to the CPS?

• Do you think those investigating the offence had already made an assumption that a CPS prosecutor was unlikely to reach a positive charging decision so had either consciously or unconsciously self-limited the extent of the investigation?

• If you have answered yes, think now how your bias and assumptions influenced your investigative mindset and decision making?

What if a child or young person is a genuine victim of trafficking for county lines exploitation but because of your prior experience and investigative mindset you've sought only to seek out evidence that supports your grounds to suspect that they are involved in drug supply? Think about the primary role of a police officer and your duty to protect and safeguard the most vulnerable. Does the approach of only identifying evidence to support a prosecution conflict with your duty as a police officer?

• If yes, how does this approach conflict with your role and responsibilities as a police officer?

• If no, set out your reasons for adopting this approach.

Conducting an effective investigation

Confirmation bias in the context of selectively searching for evidence to support your sus-picion or theory that a person has committed the offence presents a real and very pre-sent risk to public confidence in policing, and this goes to the heart of our criminal justice system. With fewer police officers carrying an ever-increasing workload, it is perhaps only human that shortcuts are made and that officers do only the minimum required to support a prosecution case. However, investigative qualities such as thoroughness and open-mindedness, together with the ability to consider evidence which leads away from as well as towards a person's involvement in a crime, are all crucial to securing a just and effective investigation which will ultimately lead to a fair trial. For these reasons you need to con-stantly challenge your own thoughts and attitudes.

Confirmation bias is the tendency to seek, attend to and interpret information in a way that is consistent with our preconceptions, including expectations and pre-existing theories (McLean et al, 2022).

Consider the child or young person in this way: that for the upstream organisers and 'kingpins' of an OCG, they represent a cheap, easily recruited workforce who can absorb the risks related to street-level dealing and are essentially a disposable commodity (Windle et al, 2020).

The harms caused to children and young people associated with county lines are well reported (NCA, 2019). The real risk of harm, together with the risk of criminalisation as a result of their exploitation, only exasperates their plight. The concern among frontline workers is that it is still often the case that criminalisation of a child exploited to commit crime is the key response and not safeguarding (James, 2021).

When undertaking a county lines investigation, it is important that you gather from the outset all the available information, intelligence and evidence to identify whether an indi-vidual is a victim of modern slavery. There are many reasons why a potential victim may choose to reveal or conceal the extent of their vulnerability and exploitation. Regardless of their status, a thorough investigation, together with an understanding of the modern slavery law and an awareness of the county lines exploitation indicators, will make it easier to iden-tify the victims of modern slavery and distinguish them from lower-level drug dealers.

You will need to have consideration for any subsequent investigation and in particular:

- show the attribution between the potential victim, offender and facilitation/arrangement of the victim's travel;
- show why the child was chosen. Evidence can include the child's vulnerabilities;
- gather all the available evidence, intelligence and information from all police forces, local authorities and other partners in which the child has, or has been known to, come to notice;
- evidence changes in behaviour and whether the child has sustained recent injuries.
(summarised from College of Policing, 2021)

Police officers need to proactively consider the presence of trafficking for the purpose of exploitation when investigating offences linked to county lines. They need to be consist-ently looking for the indicators of exploitation. Wherever possible, those investigating these offences should not focus solely on the evidence of the potential victim but seek out and obtain independent evidence in respect of their exploitation and prove other essential elements of the offence.

While balancing the needs of the investigation with the immediate safeguarding needs of the potential victim, you will also be cognisant of the intelligence and evidential opportunities that might be presented which may assist in identifying those 'upstream' who are responsible for organising, exploiting and directing that child to sell drugs on the street. These crimes are always challenging to investigate. It is therefore crucial that all available opportunities to gather intelligence and/or secure evidence are taken.

To assist the police and wider law enforcement, a multi-agency county lines co-ordination centre has been established, bringing together officers from the NCA and policing to develop intelligence and take action against the most serious offenders. It is crucial that you gather all the relevant available information to assist your local intelligence teams to understand what is happening on the streets of your towns and cities so that a clear intelligence picture can be developed that will lead to a law enforcement response. It is also important that you understand your force guidance for submitting intelligence.

Key points

- It is unlikely that you will know a child's journey or how they came to be involved in county lines. Take time to understand: their timeline will tell you far more than the details of the offence you are investigating.

- Maintain an open mind and be live to the presence of confirmation bias and how it can influence your decision making.

- Understand the practical application of the law (Modern Slavery Act 2015) when dealing with those involved in county lines drugs supply.

- Be thorough in your approach and look away from as well as towards a person's involvement; this is your best chance of coming to the right criminal justice outcome.

Part 3

Mindset, choices and priorities: investigative decision making

Chapter 5
Achieving best evidence: assault of an elderly adult

Learning objectives

By the end of this chapter you should be able to:

• explain the importance of planning to your decision making;

• explain the ways in which your decision making may be impacted by workplace influences;

• describe the key elements of an investigative mindset;

• apply the national decision model to support an investigation.

Introduction

This chapter explores an assault in the street and the initial evidence gathering from the victim. It examines the characteristics of an investigative mindset and how applying it can help you gather the best evidence. The chapter works through key elements of the national decision model, exploring how the application of policy, procedure and an investigative mindset can help you make effective and justifiable decisions.

Scenario

Jenny is working on an investigation team that deals with investigations that have a named offender that are at PIP1 level (volume and priority crime). She has been allocated an investigation where a 70-year-old man phoned the police two days ago to report that he had been assaulted. The initial call log indicates that he had been walking to his local shops when he saw a young man drop some litter. He approached the man to tell him to pick it up and they exchanged some words where the man was verbally aggressive, swearing at the victim. As the victim tried to walk away the man pushed him, causing him to stumble and fall over; the man laughed and picked up the victim's walking stick and threw it in a nearby bin.

→

The victim has sustained several small cuts and bruising to his hands and knees. He recognised the man as living on the same estate and he has frequently seen him walk past his house with a group of other men. When he saw the local shopkeeper, he told him what had happened and described the man. The shopkeeper said it sounded like a man called Dylan Allaston who was banned from the shop for stealing items and anti-social behaviour. He also said that he had seen Dylan outside the shop about 20 minutes ago. The shopkeeper showed the victim a photo of the man from his 'banned' sheet and the victim recognised him. Jenny's supervisor has allocated her the case and asked her to make contact with the victim and to record his statement.

Jenny has been working on the team for three months and during that time she has been surprised by how busy everyone is. Every day there are a number of abstractions through illness, secondment or training and the team is also carrying several vacancies. The workload coming in every day is relentless and sometimes she feels swamped by the amount of work. When she has asked her colleagues how they manage, they have told her that sometimes you just need to go through the motions, take a statement, make an arrest and then write off the job as quickly as possible. If there is any evidential difficulty, then the case will be unlikely to proceed to a charge and minimum inquiries to get the case to a position that it can be disposed of will be undertaken.

She has dealt with many assault investigations. She feels familiar with this type of investigation, knows the processes to follow and can already see that there are likely to be evidential difficulties with the identification of the suspect. To help speed things up, she has seen many of her colleagues take statements from victims and witnesses over the telephone. Jenny is considering phoning the victim in this case and taking his statement over the phone to help her to deal with the report efficiently.

Explore your thinking

Having read the above scenario think about these initial questions.

• Do you think it is okay to take a telephone statement, and why?

• How might a telephone statement impact on the investigation?

• Explain if you think the victim could be vulnerable or intimidated in this scenario.

• How much does the behaviour of your colleagues affect what you see as acceptable practice?

Discussion

The challenge of balancing efficiency and effectiveness is a reality of contemporary policing. However, the workplace pressures you face do not lessen the need to make informed and reasoned decisions and act professionally. Stepping back from usual practice and team norms to assess what you are doing and the implications of this can be a healthy process to allow you to challenge your practice. Adopting an investigative mindset rather than a routine process-driven mindset can allow you to focus your investigations to gather the best evidence rather than just the usual evidence. This chapter therefore first explores the concept of investigative mindset before then specifically focusing on that critical first decision you are faced with: how to obtain the victim account.

Investigative mindset

An investigative mindset is the thinking that drives your decision making. At the heart of the investigative mindset is the need to remain open-minded. This means allowing yourself to be open to new information as it emerges, and to changing your thoughts and understanding of what has happened as further information is gathered. It also means that you should avoid any pre-judgements or assumptions about victims, witnesses or suspects. It involves elements of professional curiosity, which encourages you to ask questions and not take things at face value, in order to understand the source of your material and think beyond the obvious.

However, applying an investigative mindset can be challenging. You need to be aware of your own biases and assumptions so that you can understand how they might be impacting on your actions. This is covered in more detail in Chapter 1 and the principles discussed there are equally applicable to all investigations.

Similarly, the environment in which you work can also influence the way you think and act. As adults, core ways that you will learn in the workplace are through experience and through observing your colleagues (Bandura, 1971). While sometimes this may be a deliberate conscious learning process, sometimes it is an inadvertent consequence of exposure to daily working practices. In this way, your behaviours are learned through a process of modelling through deliberate or inadvertent learning from examples and behaviours of others.

Therefore, you are likely to be influenced by what you see your colleagues doing and this will influence your perception of what behaviours are correct. As a relatively new investigator, if you are exposed to poor models of behaviour then there is a risk that you can unwittingly adopt this as normal procedure. Therefore, you should challenge yourself to ask why you are making certain decisions and why you are undertaking certain actions.

The other barrier to adopting an investigative mindset is the routine and process-driven mindset. The above scenario is a relatively routine type of investigation that you may be faced with as a PIP1 investigator. It is important to recognise that repeated exposure to similar activities can impact on the way that you approach the task. Consider the following exercise to help you start to apply this.

Explore your thinking

Think back to when you first learned how to drive.

• How much concentration and effort did you have to put in to making sure your car was positioned correctly on the road, monitoring your speed, working out how hard to press the accelerator or the brake and how to change gear?

Initially these are difficult skills that can take a lot of cognitive effort to master.

Now think about your current driving ability.

• How often do you find yourself driving and not really thinking about the mechanics of changing gear, instinctively knowing the right amount of pressure to apply to the brakes or the accelerator etc?

Discussion

The more practice and exposure you have to driving, the more automatic and therefore sub-conscious your actions become. It is almost as though you don't need to think about what you are doing to make the car move, turn and stop. In this way, you have adopted habits and routine ways of driving that you are no longer having to think about. This example considers a specific skill but the principles can be applied to other examples which are routine and repeated frequently.

Establishing routines at an early stage of your career can be useful for helping to develop skills and embed practices. However, it also means that investigations can became very functional and just be seen as a process that needs to be undertaken (imagine a conveyor belt churning out standardised investigations) rather than applying an individual approach looking at the opportunities within each investigation. One of the effects of this process-driven routine behaviour developed through repeated exposure to high turnover/low-level volume crime investigations is the formation of habits. Habits are a coping mechanism and allow people to undertake actions in a routine and automatic manner (Aarts and Dijksterhuis, 2000). These habits and routines can help to make you feel more comfortable as you are dealing with what you know and are working within a known set of norms. However, routine and automatic processes can sometimes mean you stop being a *thinking investigator* and this can be a barrier to effective decision making.

Workplace pressures can also be a barrier to applying the investigative mindset as high workloads and a lack of resources mean that sometimes you may feel overwhelmed and this can result in cognitive shortcuts being taken. This means you may be more susceptible to making quick premature decisions before you have the information to make properly informed decisions. One way that this effect can be seen is in categorising investigations at an early stage and making quick assumptions about whether it is likely to proceed to charge or not. This can then influence the time and effort that you spend on a case.

Applying an investigative mindset

In the earlier scenario, if you take a process-driven approach to the investigation, assuming there are identification issues and it is unlikely to proceed to charge, then you may simply do the following:

• take a telephone statement from the victim;

• take a short statement from the shopkeeper confirming the identification;

• check if CCTV covers the location of the assault;

• interview the suspect.

However, if you apply an investigative mindset, it allows you to more broadly consider the other lines of inquiry that are unique to this particular investigation. While the identification does cause some difficulties, the interaction with the shopkeeper also provides some valuable investigative opportunities. He can place the suspect in a particular location near the crime scene at around the relevant time. This may be important if during the suspect interview the suspect says he was at home or otherwise places himself somewhere else. Similarly, the shopkeeper, or perhaps CCTV from the shop covering the area outside, may be able to provide a description of clothing. If the victim can provide a similar description (uncontaminated from discussions with the shopkeeper) then this may also be supporting evidence. Also, while the identification is of lower value than a police-conducted process, it is not without any value at all. In this way, the case can potentially be strengthened rather than viewing what happened with the shopkeeper as a block to the investigation.

It is important to recognise that this is not taking you additional time; you should be taking a statement from the shopkeeper in any case, but you are now focusing your questions more effectively to support latter decision making rather than just unthinkingly following a habitual process.

It is a conscious choice to apply an investigative mindset to move beyond subconscious and automatic thinking processes to look at the bigger picture, in order to understand what your overall aim is, to question not only the material you are gathering but to question yourself and your actions to understand what you are doing and why you are doing it. This also means asking yourself key questions when making a decision including the following.

• Can I do it?

  – What does the law, policy and guidance say?

- Should I do it?

  - How will it help me achieve the aims of the investigation?

  - Does it help me to gather the best evidence?

  - How might it impact on the investigation?

This chapter now looks at how applying the investigative mindset in the context of the national decision model can really support you in making effective and proportionate decisions.

Gathering information and intelligence

Within this investigation, the first decision you are faced with is how you are going to obtain the victim's account. On the face of it this may appear straightforward and you may simply be asking yourself: shall I take a statement over the phone or face to face? However, when engaging with any victim or witness you should be asking yourself three initial questions.

1. How will this person be able to provide their best evidence?

2. Does this person have any other needs that should be addressed to support them through the criminal justice process?

3. What information can the person provide about:

    - the actual offence (eg what happened during the assault);

    - other investigative information (eg previous knowledge of the offender, who else has handled the walking stick as this may be relevant if you were considering fingerprinting).

Therefore, before you engage with any victim or witness, outside of a real-time situation, you should undertake some form of planning so that you are targeting your questioning appropriately and gathering the right kind of information to support your investigation.

So, within this scenario before you even start asking the questions to complete the victim statement you need to have gathered information to help you address the first two points above. Your initial contact plan should involve seeking information about the victim in order to establish the best ways to gather their evidence and also the best way to support them through the criminal justice system. This is an initial assessment to gather information to allow you to make the best decision about how to obtain the victim's evidence. This is important for an effective investigation because you want to try to achieve the best evidence.

Explore your thinking

Think of some older people that you know or have known, perhaps someone in their 60s, someone in their 70s or someone 80 years and over. For each of them consider the following questions.

- What are/were their cognitive functions like?
- Do/did they have any physical ailments or disabilities?
- Do/did they have mobility issues?
- Do/did they have difficulties understanding or communicating and what are/were the reasons for this (eg dementia, hearing loss, eyesight problems, loss of teeth/poorly fitted denture etc)?
- How well can/could they remember and recount events (fading memory, confusion)?

Discussion

If you were now able to compare your answers with someone else doing this exercise, it is likely that you would have a range of different characteristics listed even within each age range. Some people in their 60s are less mobile, have more cognitive difficulties and more disabilities than people in their 90s, who can sometimes be spritely, keen of mind, physically healthy and suffer no significant illness. Your perception of what older people can or cannot do can sometimes be drawn from your own experiences and this can lead to assumptions.

The point of this exercise is that older people cannot be treated as a homogenous group. They are individuals and will have individual needs that should be assessed on a case-by-case basis. It is important that you do not make assumptions about a person based on their age: either that they are only in their 60s or early 70s and therefore will be fine, or that because they are older they will have vulnerabilities and won't be able to provide as accurate and reliable information as a younger person can. Both assumptions are problematic. This is all about gathering information to establish how the victim can provide their best evidence, so you need to consider the individual abilities and circumstances of the victim on a case-by-case basis.

Furthermore, the Code of Practice for Victims of Crime (Ministry of Justice, 2020) says that victims should be given a victim needs assessment. Part of this is to establish whether there are any safeguarding concerns and what other support they may need outside of the primary evidence-gathering procedures. There are 12 rights that you should familiarise yourself with and two that specifically warrant attention for this chapter:

1. the right to be referred to services that support victims and to have needs assessed so services and support can be tailored to those needs;

2. the right to be provided with information, updates and told when important decisions are made.

If a victim is defined as vulnerable or intimidated then they have enhanced rights, so for example any victim should be updated within five working days when key decisions are made, but for those eligible for enhanced rights this is reduced to one day.

Explore your thinking

• Why do you think it is important to refer people to victim support services?

• Why do you think it is important to keep victims updated in a timely manner?

Discussion

Crimes can affect victims in different ways and it is important that you do not make assumptions about how you think someone should be feeling after they have reported a crime. While the incident may seem trivial or routine for you, for the victim this may be a really significant event. The HMCPSI and HMICFRS (2019) acknowledge that as people age they can become more aware that they are slowing down mentally and physically and of their vulnerabilities. They may also be more isolated and lack the support network of friends, colleagues or family that younger people may encounter on a daily basis. This can lead to the crime having a disproportionate effect on them. They may feel more scared and become reluctant to even leave their house.

Victim support services can offer appropriate support to help victims cope with what has happened and assist in them regaining their sense of normality. Sometimes just knowing that there is someone to talk to can make a difference. Visit the Victim Support website at www.victimsupport.org.uk for more information on the services that are available. This service also means that the victim's emotional needs are being met by an appropriate service, allowing you to focus on the investigation. Research indicates that when an older person feels supported and protected then they are less likely to disengage from the criminal justice process (HMCPSI and HMICFRS, 2019).

Similarly, just keeping people updated can make them feel valued and that they are being taken seriously. Again, this can help them to feel more engaged with the criminal justice system and also more likely to report something to the police again. At its heart, this supports the notion of procedural justice and policing by consent that was discussed in Chapter 1.

Sometimes victim assessments are not completed at all and even where they are, sometimes they can be approached as a tick-box exercise. Research has also found that older people are not asked relevant questions to identify vulnerabilities (Britain Thinks, 2019). Within this scenario, when you are gathering information from the victim it is not merely about gathering their age, as by itself that does not really tell you anything useful, but you should be considering whether the person may be vulnerable or intimidated and how that may impact on the way you will gather their evidence. While age alone does not define vulnerability for an older person, you should be considering whether there is higher likelihood of mental impairment, illness or physical disability or other barriers to providing best evidence.

Explore your thinking

Revisit the earlier scenario.

• What information from it may alert you to the possibility that the victim *may* be vulnerable or intimidated?

Discussion

When considering vulnerability, you may have noted things such as his age (70 years-old) and the possibility of a physical disability (use of a walking stick). When considering whether he is an intimidated witness, you may have noted that the victim and suspect live on the same estate and the suspect walks past the victim's house so this may be a warning sign for intimidation.

Of course, none of these points on their own mean that the victim is vulnerable or intimidated, but they should start you thinking about the possibility. This will then allow you to direct your questions and your initial assessment to help you answer these questions. In this way, initial assessments should be tailored to the individual and the individual circumstances to help you gather evidence appropriately rather than blandly gathering information about someone that is of no practical relevance.

When gathering information at this early stage, you should also consider the victim's wishes. Research on behalf of the HMCPSI and HMICFRS conducted by Britain Thinks (2019) found that older victims preferred to have a statement taken in person and to have face-to-face contact with a police officer. This helped them to feel supported and reassured that the police were taking their case seriously and helped them to engage more fully in the criminal justice process. Of course, it is not always possible or practicable to meet a victim's wishes but nevertheless this should still form part of the decision-making process.

Part of your information gathering should also be seeking information that allows you to establish if there are any safeguarding concerns, risks or additional support that the victim may need. Some of these issues will therefore specifically be considered in the second part of the decision model.

Assessing threat and risk and developing a working strategy

Of course, one of your primary concerns should always be an immediate assessment of risk and threat and this should be reviewed regularly. In the previous section, it was identified that the victim lives on the same estate as the suspect and the victim sees him walk past his house. In this case there does not appear to be an immediate risk to the victim, but this would need to be revisited as the investigation progressed, especially following the interview if the suspect identifies who has made a complaint against him. There are potential risks of intimidation in the future or repeat offending against the victim. Therefore, ensuring the victim has your contact details and providing information about what to do if there are any problems, as well as some reassurance, may be sufficient in the immediacy but should be reviewed as the case progresses.

Considering powers and policies

The information that you gather during the first part of the model should aim to help you to determine whether the victim falls into a category defined under the Youth Justice and Criminal Evidence Act (YJCEA) 1999 as section 16 vulnerable or section 17 intimidated. If they do, then you need to think about how this may impact on the quality of the evidence and the way that it should be gathered and presented.

Remember that all interviews are about obtaining accurate and reliable information so you should be aiming to maximise the opportunities to achieve this. The Ministry of Justice (2022) publication *Achieving Best Evidence* provides detailed guidance about how to do this. If the victim is deemed as vulnerable (section 16) or intimidated (section 17) then you need to make sure you are gathering their evidence in the best way, perhaps through a video-recorded interview, making sure that you are asking questions in an appropriate manner and perhaps engaging with appropriate specialists to support effective communication such as a registered intermediary.

The information you have gathered also allows you to identify any special measures or adjustments that may be required at court to help the victim to provide evidence. As well as some of the more obvious special measures such as providing their evidence in chief through a video-recorded interview, this might also include the use of hearing loops or seeking permission for the victim to provide their evidence seated rather than standing. All of this helps the court to be able to hear the best evidence available by removing or managing hurdles towards providing it.

Given the decision you are faced with, you also need to consider what the guidance says about whether you can take a telephone statement. It is legally acceptable to take a statement over the telephone (CPS, nd) but you need to ask yourself if it is the right way to gather best evidence and under what circumstances you could consider it and when you should avoid it. Kent Police (2021) have issued guidance for their officers which you may find helpful. They emphasise that face-to-face statements should be the starting point for any decision making. So, to move away from this would require clear, well-reasoned grounds. While it is recognised that telephone statements may offer an efficient and timely way of gathering evidence, the decision to use them must be carefully considered and clear rationale recorded in line with any other decision that you make in an investigation. They specifically say that telephone interviews are not suitable when:

• there are identified vulnerabilities;

• the victim/witness prefers a face-to-face interview;

• the quality of the evidence could be diminished if it is not taken face to face.

They may be suitable if:

• the quality of the evidence will not be diminished through a telephone interview;
• the victim/witness is out of the county, there are impending deadlines to be met, and it is not practicable to travel or task the statement to another force;
• personal safety factors exist (eg Covid-19 shielding).

It is these considerations that should underpin your decision making about whether a telephone statement is the right way to obtain the best evidence from the victim rather than merely what you have seen your colleagues doing. Under Covid-19 restrictions, the use of telephone statements necessarily increased and perhaps became standard process, but it is precisely this kind of process that you should be questioning and asking if it is really helping you to achieve the aims of your investigation.

Identifying options and contingencies

As part of your planning, you have now thought about the questions you need to ask to identify whether there are any vulnerabilities that may affect the victim providing the best evidence. You have thought about how you can provide support for the victim through a needs assessment and referral to victim support. You have also considered whether there may be risks of intimidation and how you could manage that. You are aware of the YJCEA 1999 and the special measures that may be applicable. You are also aware of the guidance around taking telephone statements.

Therefore, your plan should now identify what your options and contingencies are. If the information you gather identifies that the victim is vulnerable (under section 16) then you may decide that conducting a video-recorded interview and utilising specialist support to aid communication is the best approach.

If the victim reports that he feels scared and worried about reprisals, then you should conduct a risk assessment and ascertain what action you can take; this may range from providing reassurance, a point of contact, a patrol car to drive past when available or consideration of crime prevention advice. You should also plan to keep this under review.

If from the information you gather you are satisfied that a statement is the appropriate way of obtaining the victim's account, then you need to decide if a telephone statement is the best option. Having taken the victim's wishes and the guidance into account, you also need to apply your investigative mindset. Is taking a telephone statement depriving you of opportunities for gathering further evidence? For example, in this case, the victim has sustained injuries so seeing them face to face may allow you to record the injuries properly rather than merely perhaps relying on emailed copies of photos taken by the victim. A face-to-face interview with an older person may allow you to develop better rapport and allow them more time to consider and respond to your questions than can be achieved in a telephone interview. Always think about what is the best evidence that can be obtained. So, in this case it would appear inappropriate to take a telephone statement as the rationale would be as a time-saving measure rather than being the most effective measure of gathering the best evidence.

Of course, there is always a balance to be met and it may be that there are practical limitations such as you do not have access to a vehicle due to other operational commitments. This does not mean that you should automatically fall back on obtaining a telephone statement though. As a contingency, you could phone the victim to introduce yourself and ask if they are able and willing to attend the police station to allow you to complete their statement. However, it needs to be explained that it is a free choice and you should not manipulate them as for some people this may be difficult or undesirable. You could also consider whether a video call would be appropriate instead. Whichever way, the point is that you should consider your options to try to gather the best evidence in a reasonable and proportionate manner and be able to justify that decision.

Summary

You may be reading through this thinking that there is a lot to think about when making a simple decision about whether to take a telephone statement or not. However, in reality this should be part of your planning process when you are first allocated the case. You should always be thinking about who the victim is, how you can best gather their evidence and what the consequences are of your choices. The above discussion breaks it down to get you to apply the investigative mindset to the decision making rather than just doing what you have seen your colleagues do or what seems easiest.

You haven't created additional work as you will be taking a statement anyway; you should be doing a victim needs assessment, including identifying any risk, and a referral to victim support should always be made in appropriate cases. All you are doing is applying a structure to focus your questions and the information you are gathering to support witness engagement, victim satisfaction and confidence, and to try to ensure you are gathering the best evidence.

Key points

- All victims and witnesses should be treated as individuals and no assumptions should be made which may impact on your decision making.

- Learning from your colleagues is a powerful influence on your own decision making and actions.

- Be aware of falling into routine and habitualised behaviours where you adopt a process-oriented mindset.

- Policies and procedures should be used to support your decision making.

- Adopting an investigative mindset supports effective and justified decision making.

Further reading

The College of Policing has conducted a rapid evidence assessment to help to develop guidelines to support the application of an investigative mindset. The consultation document can be found as detailed below. Once the consultation is complete, the final document will be available on the College of Policing website so you should look for that when it is available.

College of Policing (2022) *Conducting Effective Investigations: Guidelines: Consultation.* [online] Available at: https://assets.college.police.uk/s3fs-public/2022-07/Conducting-effective-investigations-guidelines.pdf (accessed 31 March 2023).

Chapter 6
Getting off to the right start: responding to sexual assault

Learning objectives

By the end of this chapter you should be able to:

- recognise how a trauma-informed approach will improve a victim's account;

- understand how your communication can impact a victim's decision to support the investigation;

- identify early evidential opportunities and their relevance to a positive criminal justice outcome;

- identify factors that influence your decision making.

Introduction

This chapter examines how your decisions as the first officer attending a victim of a sexual offence can impact on the rest of the investigation. How you interact with a victim during your initial contact may influence their decision to support the investigation, even during its early stages. The chapter explores how adopting a more compassionate supportive approach will benefit the immediate investigative response, commonly referred to as the 'Golden Hour', including what actions and decisions need to be made at pace. It discusses how speaking to a victim in an inappropriate manner, using 'victim-blaming' language, or giving the victim the sense that you doubt the truthfulness of what they say are reasons often given by victims when asked why they did not support a police investigation.

The chapter uses a fictional scenario to explore your thoughts while considering the procedural and evidential steps to be taken. You are encouraged to look at how a more trauma-informed approach can generate an empathic style to aid the development of early rapport. Negative attitudes and behaviours which commonly impact this type of investigation are explored, including societal biases, stereotyping, compassionate fatigue and how an increase in crime reporting often leads officers to consider at an early stage that a victim's account is fabricated or false.

Finally, the chapter explores how by adopting a more victim-centred approach you can maximise the quality of their evidence while identifying wider supportive and corroborative evidential opportunities, together with identifying other investigative lines of inquiry. It discusses the importance of appropriate questioning and accurate record keeping and how the defence may seek to exploit the absence of detail in note taking or poor questioning to challenge the truthfulness and accuracy of a victim's recollection.

Scenario

During a busy late shift and 45 minutes before going off duty, I was on patrol with a more senior colleague when we were directed to a report of a woman who had phoned the police to say that she had been sexually assaulted. My colleague said that this was a typical weekend call where a young woman gets very drunk, meets someone and then finds herself in a situation where she can't really remember what happened, or who said or did what, and because she is embarrassed she tells everyone that she's the victim of a sexual assault. It was clear to me that they weren't really interested.

As we drove to the scene, I began to think about the 'Golden Hour' and what I needed to consider:

• whether there would be any immediate medical or safeguarding needs;

• whether the use of a body-worn camera would be appropriate;

• separating witnesses;

• early evidence kit;

• where the suspect might be.

I felt almost overwhelmed at the thought of all the things I might have to do. I really wanted to get it right, not just for the victim but also because our force was placing extra scrutiny on the actions of first officers attending sexual offences. I didn't want negative comments aimed at me at the start of my career. At one point I found myself thinking that I could just stand back and leave it to my colleague; they were more senior and should know what to do – if there's criticism later it's nothing to do with me.

Once we arrived at the scene, I saw the victim sitting on the pavement. Her clothing was disheveled, she was crying and her blouse was open, exposing her bra. I held back hoping my colleague would step forward but they were already on the radio updating comms. They ushered me forward.

I remembered my training and about doing the basics well. I spoke to the victim with a calm reassuring tone as I wanted her to feel comfortable in my presence. I allowed her time to calm down, and even though it was only a few minutes I felt like I was slowly gaining her trust. Once I could see that her emotional state was stabilising and there were no immediate medical or safeguarding needs, I began to obtain a first account from her of what had happened. She said that earlier that evening she had met a man in a pub, that they'd got on well and had left together. He asked if he could walk her home. Once off the main High Street, he asked for a kiss. Before she could reply, he pushed her against a wall, kissed her, forced his hand into her underwear and digitally penetrated her before trying to rip away her underwear. I listened intently. Once I'd obtained her account, we drove the victim to the Sexual Assault Referral Centre (SARC).

Afterwards, my colleague said how impressed they were with how I'd dealt with the situation. I'd always been interested in this area of work, which is probably why I remembered my training; however, I knew of colleagues who would do anything to avoid attending these offences. What if one of those officers had attended? Might the victim have had a completely different experience, and what effect might that have had on the quality of the initial account and the investigation?

Explore your thinking

- Do you think that a police officer's decision making can be influenced by their biases and stereotyping of a victim, particularly those that appear intoxicated, resulting in negative assumptions as to the truthfulness of a report of sexual assault?

  – If yes, how might these types of negative attitudes present?

  – If no, think of occasions where positive qualities were demonstrated. How did these officers interact with the victim?

  – How might a police officer's perception of a victim who has reported a sexual assault when intoxicated influence their approach to the initial response?

  – What are the risks of allowing biases and stereotyping to affect a police officer's investigative mindset, particularly in cases involving sexual assault?

  – Do you think that police officers have sufficient knowledge about how sexual violence affects a victim's presentation and their ability to remember and recall what they have experienced?

You will likely have experienced meeting victims of sexual violence. Therefore, you will know how very differently victims who have experienced sexual violence can present. This chapter examines your thinking and your actions, and the positive and potentially detrimental impact that your decisions can have as the first officer attending.

Contemporary issues in policing: sexual offences

In recent years, much criticism has been levelled at policing and its approach to dealing with victims of sexual violence, as well as the quality of criminal investigations (HMICFRS, 2021c). This criticism is set against a backdrop in which the entire criminal justice system continues to fail victims of sexual violence, particularly victims of rape (CJJI, 2022).

National crime recording saw the highest number ever of rape and sexual offences for the year ending June 2022 with 196,889 offences reported. This was a 21 per cent increase from the year ending March 2020. Of all sexual offences recorded in the year ending March 2022, 36 per cent were rape offences (ONS, 2022b) with only 1.6 per cent of rape offences resulting in someone being charged with the offence (HM Government, 2021).

The sheer scale and prevalence of sexual violence was brought to the forefront of policing as a result of a number of failed cases and high-profile investigations, some with tragic consequences. The kidnap, rape and murder of Sarah Everard in March 2021 was one such case. While operating under the cover of enforcing Covid-19 restrictions Wayne Couzens, an off-duty police officer, detained Sarah before handcuffing her and driving her away. Her body was found several days later some 70 miles away from where she had been abducted. The subsequent and understandable public and political outcry became the catalyst for change.

In June 2021, HM Government published the *End-to-end Rape Review* report, which made a number of recommendations including the launch of projects to test innovative ways for the police and CPS to investigative rape cases. Operation Soteria was one such project. It brought together leading academics and the National Police Chiefs' Council (NPCC) to form a collaborative programme of research and transformational change aimed at increasing the number of rape cases making it to court. The foundation of the project built in an emphasis on the importance of good policing practice in key areas, including adopting a suspect-focused approach and improving the quality of a victim's evidence.

Victim confidence and crime reporting

There are likely many reasons why victims of sexual violence don't report to the police. Data for the year ending March 2021 recorded that less than 20 per cent of victims of rape report to the police. Although it is widely accepted that it is the criminal justice system as a whole that has failed victims of sexual violence, much of the literature discusses the shortcomings of the police in how they manage victims and the investigation process (HM Government, 2021).

Research into rape survivors' experience of the police and other criminal justice agencies noted that nearly everyone had initial reservations about reporting their experience (CJJI, 2021). Concerns expressed included:

• worries about negative reactions from others, such as blame and stigmatisation;

• the legal system and a fear of not being believed or taken seriously;

• not viewing the incident as rape, particularly if the perpetrator was someone they knew;

• fear of reprisal from the suspect and concerns about 'ruining their life' (para 4).

Explore your thinking

• Think about what these victims have said here. How does this relate to your own experience when engaging with victims?

• How might a negative interaction with a police officer on first contact affect the quantity and quality of information provided by the victim?

Remember that adopting a kind, empathetic approach is likely to result in a more positive experience for the victim. Conversely, adopting a judgemental, disbelieving, 'robotic' approach which lacks empathy is likely to generate a negative interaction with the victim.

As the first officer attending, good investigative practice and an empathic approach are central to improving victim experience. This positive interaction is likely to lead to an increase in the quantity and quality of evidence obtained from a victim, which will ultimately increase the chances of securing convictions against those that perpetrate these types of crimes. Good decision making about how best to engage on first contact with a victim of sexual violence is therefore crucial.

The law: consent and reasonable belief in consent

Section 74 of the Sexual Offences Act 2003 provides the statutory definition of consent: 'a person consents if he agrees by choice, and has the freedom and capacity to make that choice'. Assuming that the victim had both the freedom and capacity to consent, the crucial question is often whether the victim agreed to the sexual act by choice.

The law also considers consent from the suspect's perspective and whether they had reasonable belief that the other was consenting. The test of reasonable belief is a subjective test with an objective element.

• Did the suspect genuinely believe that the victim was consenting?

• If so, did the suspect reasonably believe it?

The definition of consent can be considered in two parts, the first relating to the victim and the second to the suspect. To secure a prosecution it's not sufficient that the victim said that they did not consent. The police must gather evidence to prove that the suspect did not reasonably believe that the victim was consenting. The absence of reasonable belief can be difficult to prove, particularly where the victim is heavily intoxicated and as a result their memory of what took place is impaired.

Intoxication and consent

Section 74 makes it clear that the victim must have the capacity (the ability) to make a choice about whether to consent or not. Dependent on the amount of alcohol voluntarily consumed, it may still be possible for a victim to consent even if they had consumed a significant amount. Drunken consent is still consent if the victim remains capable of choosing whether or not to have intercourse (*R v Bree*, 2007).

The difficulty for investigators is the extent to which alcohol impairs memory. The quality of a victim's evidence, including its completeness and accuracy, will frequently be key to any decision about whether to prosecute or not. That said, you must not solely focus on the victim but also look closely at the suspect. In the circumstances, if you are able to prove the absence of reasonable belief then the offence is likely to be made out.

Explore your thinking

- Think about occasions when you have consumed a significant amount of alcohol; how was your memory affected? How clearly could you remember events from the previous evening, who you spoke to, what you said, what you did or how you got home? How often have you woken up with only a vague recollection of the previous evening? Think about occasions where you have taken a taxi home or a friend has given you a lift and you've given them directions, and in the morning you only have a vague snapshot memory of the drive home with very little detail of what was said or done.

- Think about the victim in this scenario; she too had consumed a significant amount of alcohol and was drunk. How might her recollection of what she said or did be affected by and, importantly, how might it have impacted what she may have consented to or not?

- Think about an occasion where you have responded to a similar report, where a victim said that because of how drunk they were, and with the absence of any recollection of what happened, they believe that they wouldn't have had the capacity or ability to consent and therefore any sexual activity was non-consensual.

- Now consider this from the suspect's perspective. When interviewed, the suspect said that the victim was a willing participant and that there was nothing about his interaction with her last night that made him think for one moment that she wasn't consenting. He said that the fact she couldn't remember consenting didn't make him a rapist. Do both the victim and suspect have a point here?

It is for this reason that officers and investigators must maintain an open mind and with an unbiased investigative mindset explore all reasonable and relevant lines of inquiry that point away from a suspect's guilt as well as towards it (CPIA, 1996).

- As the first officer attending, the decisions you make may be crucial in proving or disproving the complaint. Think now about the scenario and what investigative actions you as the first officer attending might consider and why; write down your thoughts and considerations.

In this, we explore the evidential opportunities rape and serious sexual offences present and how best to secure all the available evidence. From the notes that you have made here you will have the opportunity to compare your thoughts, considerations and decisions against the investigative suggestions mentioned later.

Due to the challenges these types of investigations present, it is crucial that first officers attending quickly identify opportunities to secure supportive and corroborative evidence which go beyond the 'he said, she said'. It is here that the foundations to a strong case can be laid, especially when a victim's testimony can't always be fully relied upon as in cases where a victim is heavily intoxicated and their memory is impaired.

Developing a trauma-informed approach

Sexual violence encompasses acts that range from verbal harassment to forced penetration, and an array of types of coercion, from social pressure and intimidation to physical force (World Health Organization, 2012). There are lots of different types of sexual violence, including child sexual abuse, rape and sexual assault. In other words, any kind of sexual activity or act that takes place without consent (Rape Crisis, 2022).

The resulting psychological, emotional and physical harm caused may last for many years, leaving the victim with a range of complex trauma-related symptoms. There is no hierarchy in trauma; a victim of a less serious offence isn't more or less susceptible to developing traumatic symptoms than a victim who has been raped.

The body's physiological reaction when faced with a sense of danger or threat is to respond typically in five ways. The first three, *fight*, *flight* and *freeze*, are well documented and reflect our ingrained survival instinct (Levine, 1997). Two other responses to the detection of a threat are *friend* and *flop* (Lodrick, 2007). Often referred to as the five Fs, these trauma responses are commonly referenced by those providing support to victims of sexual violence (Rape Crisis, 2022).

As survival strategies, *fight*, *flight* and *freeze* are fairly self-explanatory. The *friend* response is likely to be an unconscious attempt to engage the suspect as the person causing the sense of threat. The *flop* response occurs when the *freeze* mechanism fails and the body and mind go into a state where any impact, either physically or psychologically, will be felt less (Lodrick, 2007).

Rape myths and stereotyping are often influenced by an officer's own attitudes and beliefs about how a victim reacted to being assaulted (Gekoski et al, 2023). From a police officer's perspective, if a victim fights back or flees an assault there is an objective test that they can apply:

• is there evidence of physical injury to the victim or the perpetrator?

• is there CCTV evidence or witnesses who saw or heard the victim's attempt to run away?

Experience tells us that police officers are more likely to believe from the outset that an offence has occurred when the victim responded in either of these ways.

However, if a victim were to *freeze, flop* or *friend*, then it is these trauma responses which appear to officers to be more subjective and will often lead them to speculate about the victim's actions: *Why didn't she run away? Why didn't she fight back? Why didn't she tell him to stop? Why did she just lie there?* The risk here is that if these thoughts translate into words and a victim is asked inappropriate questions, it can leave them with a sense that they did something wrong or were to blame for what happened.

First officers attending victims of sexual violence need to be aware that what they say and how they say it can have both a positive and negative impact on the victim. Although some victims of sexual violence report positively on their interaction with the police, other victims describe their interactions differently with some feeling disbelieved and judged, or that the police lacked empathy, leaving them feeling unsupported and uncared for, but also re-victimised (CJJI, 2021).

It is perhaps for this reason that national police training places emphasis on the importance of building and maintaining a good rapport with victims of sexual violence. As the first officer attending when the victim is recounting what has happened, whether the report is about something that is recent or non-recent, the victim may still be traumatised. It is crucial that you manage your communication in a way that gives the victim the confidence to speak to you (College of Policing, 2019).

A trauma-informed approach starts with identifying the signs of trauma. How does the victim physically appear to you when you first meet? Are they upset and crying, shaking and trembling or are they sitting quietly with their head down not saying anything?

Don't ask the question directly but as you engage the victim to elicit their first account, try to identify whether one or more of the five Fs is present. Recognising their threat response will help you understand why the victim acted in the way that they did, and why they are responding to you now in the way that they are. You will be able to adapt your communication style to create an environment and atmosphere in which the victim feels more safe and trusts you. Once you have achieved this, you can move on to obtaining their first account. By taking time to respond to the traumatic effects of the sexual assault you will likely create a sense of emotional stabilisation, which will generate an increase in the quantity and quality of information provided. It is also likely to leave the victim feeling believed, supported and taken seriously.

The investigative value of a properly obtained initial account

A record of a properly obtained first account can add significant investigative value and also add weight to a victim's evidence. Conversely, a poorly obtained account can potentially undermine the investigation from commencement. This is particularly so in sexual offence investigations where an offence is committed behind a closed door where there are no witnesses and where the suspect is free to exert violence, power and control over their victim in ways that leave no physical marks or injuries.

Unlike many other crimes, with rape and other sexual offences it is often the case that the only direct evidence available is what the victim and suspect have said about what took place. Given that so much prosecutorial weight rests on the evidence of the victim, it is perhaps understandable that the defence will seek to attack and undermine the victim at every opportunity. It is crucial therefore that officers and investigators at every stage of the investigative process strive to achieve the highest investigative standards.

Police officers, like all people including jury members, are prone to making assumptions and stereotyping. However, the coercive impact that a false assumption can have on an investigation can lead to it being undermined from commencement. A common assumption among officers occurs when a victim is inconsistent or inaccurate, or when information is omitted which leads them to question the veracity or truthfulness of a victim's account.

Those investigating sex offences have often placed too much emphasis on the inconsistencies and inaccuracies in a victim's account, leading them to question the overall credibility of the victim's complaint. There are many reasons why a victim might withhold information. It may be that they were simply embarrassed and didn't want to tell a male officer that they had been raped anally, or a victim might say '*I thought if I told you the truth you wouldn't believe me*'. Equally, officers have to be aware that there are occasions, albeit rare, when a person might fabricate an account or make a wholly false report.

A crucial aim in any investigation is to establish whether a victim, or witness, is telling the truth or is giving accurate evidence. In considering witness testimony, the law assesses both the credibility and reliability of their evidence, and the weight of that evidence, and in doing so it asks whether the witness is truthful (credibility) in their account and if they are accurate (reliability) in their recollection. When assessing victim evidence, it is important to understand that when a victim is inaccurate in their recollection it doesn't mean that they are being untruthful or that they have chosen to be selective about what information they reveal. A victim may genuinely believe that they are being truthful in their recollection but other investigative material such as CCTV contradicts their version of what happened.

You may have experienced this when you have reviewed your body-worn video following an incident, comparing your memory of what you thought had happened to what actually happened as recorded. A victim of sexual violence is no different; they won't always remember events accurately, particularly immediately after the incident. This is why it is important that you understand how trauma affects memory as this knowledge will inform how you engage with a victim and obtain their first account.

Obtaining the first account

The terminology used to describe the record of what a witness said to an officer varies, with terms such as obtaining a 'brief', 'initial' or 'first' account commonly used. For consistency, the witness or victim account provided to an officer on first contact is referred to as the first account.

The first account is intended to elicit a brief explanation of what took place to determine whether an offence has taken place, if it has, what offence has been committed and what immediate investigatory action needs to be taken. Officers should not ask questions beyond what information they need to know to identify any immediate safeguarding, medical and investigative action. When obtaining the first account, allow the victim to speak freely about what has happened. Do not stop the recall of significant events related to the offence under investigation. Where you can, use open questions such as 'tell me' to elicit information and establish:

• what has happened;

• who did it;

• where it happened;

• when it happened.

The answers to these questions will likely influence any immediate action that you may need to take to safeguard and support the victim, identify any urgent medical and forensic considerations, locate the crime scene, identify witnesses and assist with the early identification of the suspect. Only ask questions that you need to ask to understand what has taken place and ask no more questions than is necessary. A more detailed account can then be obtained during the formal interview process. Interviewing traumatised victims of sexual violence beyond obtaining a first account is a specialist skill and should not be undertaken by those who haven't had the appropriate training.

There are occasions when attending officers go beyond obtaining the first account and stray into what would normally be captured in a video-recorded interview. When this happens, they run the risk of harming the investigation. As the officer tries to elicit as much detail as possible in the belief they are acting appropriately, they inadvertently invite the victim to provide greater detail of the incident which isn't required at that point to achieve the immediate investigative actions, but which will be asked in the formal interview. The issue here is that when the same questions are asked again during the formal interview process the victim's recollection may be slightly different from what they told the officer, or the same question is phrased slightly differently prompting a change in the recount. As a consequence, and inadvertently, the victim is viewed as providing an inconsistent or inaccurate account and it will simply become an unfounded opportunity to attack the truthfulness and accuracy of the victim's recollection (Cook and Tattersall, 2014)

Explore your thinking

• Think about an occasion when you responded to a highly stressful or traumatic incident such as a violent public order situation or a fight.

• On what did your memory focus at moments of high emotional distress or stress?

• How aware were you of what was taking place at the periphery, or were you focused on what was presenting the greatest threat?

• After the incident, did you simply remember the worst moments of that event?

This type of memory encoding is often referred to as 'hotspot' and is commonly found in those that have experienced trauma, including victims of sexual violence.

Now think about the scenario in this chapter; you have a drunk woman who has said that she has been sexually assaulted. You are aware of the nature of the report prior to arrival.

• How might you record the first account?

• Will you make comprehensive notes of what questions you asked and their reply?

• Would you ask a colleague to make a detailed record so you could focus on the victim or would you use body-worn video (BWV) to record what the victim said?

• If you decided to activate your camera, what is your rationale for doing so?

• If you chose not to activate your camera, what was your rationale for doing so?

The use of body-worn video to record a first account from a victim of a sexual offence

In principle, users of body-worn video (BWV) are not required to obtain the expressed consent of any person being filmed. It is for the user to consider on a case-by-case basis whether or not to switch the BWV off (NPCC, 2022). However, applying this principle in a case of rape or serious sexual violence requires greater consideration. In such incidents, BWV may be used to record initial accounts only where the victim has consented and has the capacity to consent. The phrase commonly used when engaging with victims of sexual violence is '*informed consent*' (College of Policing, 2019).

In the scenario in this chapter, you are responding to a serious sexual assault. Given that the offence has only just happened the suspect could still be in the area. You know from what has already been said that the suspect might have forensic evidence on him or his clothing. You are also aware of the evidential challenges presented in cases of consent and drunkenness. You are keen to secure all available evidence, including obtaining an appropriately detailed and accurate first account.

You consider using your BWV to record the account, but before you do so, you need to consider what the implications of that decision might be. Making the decision to activate your BWV as the first officer attending a victim of sexual violence presents a number of dilemmas as you balance the needs and interests of the victim against the needs of the investigation.

Explore your thinking

• Does an intoxicated victim of sexual violence have the capacity to give their informed consent to having their initial account videoed? Yes or no?

  – If yes, what are the advantages to video recording the first account?

  – If yes, what questions are you intending to ask the victim and why?

→

- If yes and the case is charged, how might the victim feel when the footage is served on the defence for the perpetrator to view?

- If yes, might a victim if sober have made a different decision?

- If no, what evidence could be lost? Is video evidence the best evidence for showing how drunk the victim was?

- If no, how are you intending to accurately record what questions you ask and their replies?

- If no, how are you intending to describe in your witness statement how drunk the victim was, how her clothing appeared and her emotional state?

The police and CPS recognise the evidential benefits of recording first accounts of rape and serious sexual assault victims, although legal consideration is ongoing in terms of the necessity to seek informed consent to record and, if so, how that assessment, information and explanation should be provided to potentially vulnerable victims who may be entitled to special measures (NPCC, 2022).

Officers are encouraged to read their force policy to ensure compliance with the use of BWV. If a victim is considered vulnerable and a decision is made to BWV the first account, their rationale must be recorded using the national decision model. A police officer or a witness may be permitted to review their account prior to making and signing any witness statement (NPCC, 2022).

Developing a positive investigative mindset from first contact

As the first officer attending, you have a key role in determining the outcome of the investigation. Identifying evidential opportunities and securing that evidence during the 'Golden Hour' can be a significant factor in the successful outcome of a sexual offence case.

We will shortly explore why it is important to look beyond the notion of one word against the other and consider all potential evidential opportunities that may be available, and where to find them. We will examine the relevance and significance of each strand of evidence, and how each piece of evidence can support or corroborate other evidence to build a strong case.

The victim in this scenario telephoned the police to report what had just happened. What she said and how upset she may have been would have been recorded. As the first officer attending you will have seen that the victim was visibly upset and that her clothing was disturbed.

This scenario presents at least five key evidential opportunities that are available immediately before or on arrival at the scene, and before the first account is taken. On the face of it these opportunities may appear minor but in terms of the overall investigation, they are crucial in building a strong case.

1. *Evidence of early or recent complaint* – the fact that a complaint is made by the victim shortly after the offence occurred, as well as the details about it, is admissible evidence.

2. *Evidence of distress* – how the victim appeared physically and emotionally may corroborate what she said happened.

3. *Exhibit evidence* – telephone recording to police and the audio recording.

4. *Direct evidence* – what the victim said to the operator.

5. *Res gestae* – although each of the above evidential opportunities is potentially admissible in its own right, the *res gestae* rule provides an opportunity to combine some or all of these opportunities. The law in respect of *res gestae* says that '*if a statement was made by a person so emotionally overpowered by an event that the possibility of concoction or distortion can be disregarded*' (CJA, 2003, s 118(1)). *Res gestae* is frequently used by the CPS to support sexual and domestic violence cases (*R v Barnaby*, 2015).

Careful and sensitive questioning will likely elicit a victim's first recall that may provide other immediate lines of inquiry, such as identifying any immediate safeguarding or medical needs, forensic opportunities including early evidence kit swabs and two urine samples to evidence alcohol levels, photographing visible marks and recording in your notes how the injuries appear, witnesses, CCTV, digital media, and locating the scene and identifying the suspect.

Dependent on what is said, you may need to make a decision about whether to transport the victim to the Sexual Assault Referral Centre or Haven. These services provide immediate clinical and emotional support to victims of sexual violence. Think beyond just the forensic medical examination; these services are far better placed to deal with victims of sexual violence.

Key points

The main things to remember to help you make informed decisions about your approach to obtaining the first account from a victim of sexual violence are:

• no one victim will present the same – trauma isn't hierarchical;

• speak to the victim in a calm and supportive way to create a positive interaction;

• identify which of the 5 Fs the victim responded with;

• ask only those questions necessary and appropriate to achieve immediate safeguarding, medical and investigative 'Golden Hour' actions;

• accurately record what the victim says;

• recognise all the available evidential opportunities and build a strong case from first contact.

Further reading

Investigators should familiarise themselves with the College of Policing Authorised Professional Practice guidance available at: www.college.police.uk/app/major-investigation-and-public-protection/rape-and-sexual-offences

Chapter 7
Prioritising workloads: investigation planning

Learning objectives

By the end of this chapter you should be able to:

- recognise the importance of writing an investigation plan to create a strong investigative focus;

- identify how the Criminal Procedure and Investigation Act (CPIA) provides the legislative framework that will enable you to reach better and more informed decisions;

- recognise how the development of an investigative mindset will enable you to build a more proportionate, effective and efficient investigation;

- recognise the challenges and risks that impact the quality of an investigation when managing high caseloads.

Introduction

This chapter explores the challenges faced when managing multiple investigations and how adopting good investigative practice will create a more focused, timely investigation. It examines the importance of adopting good investigative practice from the outset, and why this approach will aid the development of an investigative mindset that will lead to better and more informed decision making. It also considers the issues that arise when shortcuts are taken and why failing to pursue proportionate, necessary and reasonable lines of inquiry can not only undermine the investigation but also negatively impact victim confidence in the criminal justice process.

Scenario

You are working a day shift as part of a priority crime team investigating volume crime. As you drive to work you are already thinking about the day ahead. Will there be suspects in the cells to deal with and will it be another late finish? Will your sergeant give you time to submit that case to the CPS for a charging decision? You are thinking about the victim updates that you need to make and whether you'll get the chance to review the other investigations allocated to you which you haven't had time to read through.

$\longrightarrow$

When you arrive at work your sergeant allocates you a dwelling burglary; the suspect is in custody waiting to be interviewed. The suspect was caught in the early hours of the morning shortly after a burglary was reported. They matched the clothing description and were in possession of property thought to have been stolen during the burglary. Upon arrest the suspect said that he had found the property on a playing field earlier that night and they weren't involved in the burglary. You have previously dealt with this person for the same offence. As a prolific offender, your sergeant wants this person charged and remanded. The burglar's modus operandi is to break a small pane of glass to gain entry, which was the case in this burglary. You are aware that for the past few weeks there have been police in that area due to a spike in night-time dwelling burglaries, and that it was covert officers who called in response officers to make the arrest.

You enjoy your work and want to do a good job, not just for victims but because you take pride in what you do. However, there seems to be fewer staff, workloads are increasing and you're worried that through no fault of your own you may let victims down because you don't have the time to properly investigate their crimes. This doesn't sit well with you and you want to explore whether there is a better way to manage your investigations which will make you more effective and efficient. Importantly, a new approach may also have the added benefit of reducing your stress levels.

Explore your thinking

- Do you think that setting an investigation plan can positively impact an investigator's approach to how they manage case progression effectively?

  - If yes, think of occasions when you have created an investigation plan and how that enabled you to build structure into your investigation.

  - If no, think of occasions when not setting an investigation plan has negatively impacted the way in which you were able to manage your investigation.

- Do you think that investigators have sufficient working knowledge of CPIA and how to apply the legislation to inform better management of their investigation?

  - If yes, think of occasions where you have used CPIA to inform how you write an investigation plan. How did you use the legislation and how did it benefit?

  - If no, take time to think about how you structure your investigations and how you approach writing an investigation plan.

Police training, like most areas of policing, is under huge strain: insufficient time in the curriculum, lack of experienced police tutors and relentless operational demands mean that those new to the role frequently feel overwhelmed and exposed. One resulting consequence is that police training is frequently limited to teaching 'what to do' and 'how to do it' without fully explaining 'why' we do something. This chapter explores the 'why' question in areas key to the investigation process. In particular, it examines why adopting an investigative mindset, setting the right investigation plan and developing a better understanding of CPIA will lead to a more focused, timely and proportionate investigation that will withstand supervisory and judicial scrutiny.

Contemporary policing issues: investigative crime standards and disclosure

Within policing there has been much conversation and debate on the erosion of investigative standards. In recent years there have been several high-profile cases that have either collapsed at trial (*R v Allen*, 2017, *R v Itiary*, 2017) or which have led to miscarriages of justice (Cardiff Five, 2003, Stefan Kiszko, 1992, Guildford Four, 1993). The subsequent public outcry following the collapsed trials, together with concerns about how the police and prosecution approached their legal obligations under CPIA, led to the publication in December 2020 of the revised Attorney General (AG) Guidelines on Disclosure.

The Home Secretary at that time said:

> *Proper disclosure of unused material remains a crucial part of a fair trial and is essential to avoiding miscarriages of justice. Disclosure remains one of the most important and complex issues in the criminal justice system, and it is a priority of the government to encourage improvements in disclosure practice in order to ensure the disclosure regime operates effectively, fairly, and justly.*
>
> (Attorney General's Office, 2022, p 1)

A joint inspection by His Majesty's Inspectors of the disclosure of unused material in volume Crown Court cases established that it was the prosecution team as a whole who were routinely failing to adhere to the principles of disclosure and that it wasn't just a matter for the police; the CPS were also criticised for failing to challenge poor-quality schedules and in turn providing little or no input to the police (HMCSPI and HMIC, 2017).

The events that followed the murder of Lynette White in 1988 represent one of the worst miscarriages of justice in the history of our criminal justice system. Five innocent men were prosecuted for her murder and in 1990 three of them were convicted. The convictions were quashed by the Court of Appeal in 1992. Thirteen police officers were later charged with perverting the course of justice but the investigation into these officers collapsed. In 2015 at the request of the Home Secretary, Richard Horwell QC examined the circumstances of the case. His report was published in July 2017 (Horwell, 2017).

Comments made by Richard Horwell QC in this report go to the heart of this chapter:

> *disclosure problems have blighted our criminal justice system for too long and although disclosure guidelines, manuals and policy documents are necessary, it is the mindset and experience of those who do disclosure work that is paramount.*
>
> (Horwell, 2017, p 5)

For too long police officers and investigators have associated CPIA and disclosure with the preparation of the MG6 series of forms. As a consequence, the completion of schedules has become a cataloguing exercise with little or no investigative thought given to what should or shouldn't be retained, recorded and revealed to the prosecutor, and why. It is crucial, there-fore, that officers and investigators understand the guiding principles of the Act and how to apply the legislation to each and every investigation. Disclosure should be completed in a thinking manner, in light of the issues in the case, and not simply as a schedule-completing exercise (Attorney General's Office, 2022).

The value of adopting an investigative mindset from commencement

CPIA requires the consideration of important disclosure matters long before the com-pletion of MG6 schedules is required. Indeed, most investigations will never reach the point where schedules are required to be completed. Nevertheless, there is a legal obliga-tion to consider these principles from the commencement of all criminal investigations, including:

- maintain an open mind;
- adopt a 'thinking person's' approach;
- pursue all reasonable lines of inquiry, including those that point away from as well as towards a suspect's guilt;
- retain, review, record and reveal relevant information and investigative material;
- keep a full log of decisions made and the reasons for those decisions.

Chapter 5 of the *Disclosure Manual* titled 'Reasonable Lines of Enquiry' explains that a rea-sonable line of inquiry will always involve considering the facts of and the issues in the case, including any defence raised (CPS, 2022b). It is important that any inquiry is proportionate, reasonable and necessary. This involves considerations of:

- what is expected to be found through the inquiry, to determine what is reasonable in the circumstances;
- how best to seek that information/material, taking a proportionate approach;
- being able to explain why it is needed.

These principles are also found in the 'investigative mindset', which is a term used to refer to the use of a disciplined approach that ensures the decisions made are appropriate to the case, are reasonable and can be explained to others (McLean et al, 2022).

Explore your thinking

The skill of the investigator is to determine what is reasonable, relevant and necessary in the pursuit of a proportionate investigation appropriate to the circumstances of the case, which complies with your legal obligations under CPIA while satisfying the evidential test that the CPS will want to consider.

- Think about all the potential investigative opportunities which the burglary scenario provides and write them down. At this stage don't limit yourself to local working practice or procedure; think broadly and capture all possible lines of inquiry.

- Think about these possible investigative opportunities and identify those that you consider to be your main lines of inquiry that are proportionate and necessary to prove your case.

- Think now about your rationale: why are you pursuing particular lines of inquiry? It is important that you record your reasons for not pursuing a reasonable line of inquiry as it is likely that both prosecutor and defence, for different reasons, will want to understand and explore your decision making.

- Think about the disclosure principles. What innocent explanation might the suspect give about how they came to be in the location where they were arrested in possession of property?

Discussion

The first point asked you to consider all investigative opportunities that may be available. These are your 'considerations', the things you could do. For example, you could consider a footwear tread comparison with the shoes they were wearing against the muddy tread mark found on the kitchen floor, compare fibres found at the point of entry against clothing worn by the suspect or analyse clothing for glass fragments that may have been deposited when a window was smashed to gain entry.

The second point asked you to identify what you considered were your main or key lines of inquiry that were going to prove your case, for example, a witness statement covering burglary points to prove, identification of stolen property and a clothing description of the suspect. These are often the proportionate but necessary inquiries to prove the offence.

For example, if the victim was to identify the property as stolen during the burglary, given that the suspect was arrested within 15 minutes of the burglary being reported, and answered no comment at interview, would it be proportionate to undertake costly forensic analysis? The forensic analysis remains a line of inquiry, but is it a reasonable or necessary line of inquiry at that point in time or will you wait for the conclusion of other lines of inquiry?

The final point encouraged you to maintain an open mind and to consider whether the suspect might be an innocent person. At first glance they may appear to have committed the burglary, but have they, or did they come into possession of the property by some other means?

This exercise will assist you with developing an investigative mindset by applying structure to your thought process and decision making. Become familiar with recording your decision-making process; if a case is contested, the defence will frequently focus on what you haven't done. Why, for example, did you decide not to complete house-to-house inquiries, not make a forensic submission or seize CCTV? If you have not closed these avenues down by way of explanation, it will provide the defence with an opportunity to assert that if you had pursued these other lines of inquiry you would have established that it was in fact another person and not the defendant. The defence will always find issues with an investigation; it's their job to do so, and to be expected. However, the impact of any defence challenge will be mitigated when decision making is recorded with rationale, and the investigator is able to articulate their reasoning.

What is an investigative mindset?

An investigative mindset is a term that expresses the essential features of what it is to be an investigator. An investigative mindset is a state of mind or attitude which investigators adopt, and which can be developed over time through continued use. It isn't something that you can just acquire; it requires a disciplined systematic approach to gathering and assessing information and material. Repeated application of this approach over time will enable you to harness this mindset and become a better, more informed decision maker. The investigative mindset can be broken down into the following five principles:

1. *understanding the source material;*
2. *planning and preparation;*
3. *examination;*
4. *recording and collation;*
5. *evaluation.*

(Centrex, 2005)

Within each of these five principles, the investigative mindset requires the investigator to keep an open mind and remain receptive to alternative suggestions, looking for other explanations and not becoming too focused on one or two theories or hypotheses (Cook and Tattersall, 2014). Personal qualities often presented by those that demonstrate an investigative mindset include:

- an enquiring and open mind;

- professional curiosity;

- thoroughness;

- a systematic and disciplined approach;

- being objective and rational.

Initial investigation and fast-track actions

Sometimes referred to as the 'Golden Hour', this is the early initial phase of the investigation when vital fast-track actions are completed. Typical fast-track actions include:

- locate and attend to the victim;

- locate and arrest the suspect;

- identify and protect crime scene(s);

- secure and preserve evidence;

- identify key witnesses.

Fast-track actions are defined as *'any investigative actions which, if pursued immediately, are likely to establish important facts, preserve evidence or lead to the early resolution of the investigation'* (College of Policing, 2023, p 1).

Unpicking the dilemma and decision making

Explore your thinking

- Think about the circumstances in this burglary scenario. What fast-track actions could you undertake?

- The suspect was found in possession of property thought to have been stolen during the burglary. Given the late hour and the steady stream of other emergency calls coming over the radio, would it be a reasonable line of inquiry at that point to ask the home owner to identify the property seized from the suspect?

You haven't yet finished booking the suspect into custody when an operator from the communication centre calls and asks when you will be resuming as they have a backlog of high-priority calls. What are you going to say? You know the suspect said that they'd found the property before the burglary was reported. However, your gut instinct is that the suspect is probably responsible for the burglary; you have this nagging feeling – what if they did actually find the property earlier that evening and it wasn't stolen during the burglary.

Explore your thinking

- What might the advantages be for the investigation if the victim was in a position to identify the property at that time?
- What might be the disadvantages for the investigation if viewing the property seized was delayed until the day shift picks up the handover?
- What might be the implications for the suspect if viewing the property is delayed?

Whichever decision you make, ensure that it is recorded. It may be as simple as asking the comms operator to update the log to say that due to the high number of immediate response calls you weren't able to ask the victim to view the property, or that given the explanation upon arrest you intend to establish whether the property seized was stolen from the burglary.

The importance of a good handover

The handover is likely to be your first opportunity to set out what actions and lines of inquiry have been completed and the result, and to draw attention to anything that you think is relevant to the prompt and effective investigation.

In relation to this scenario, the handover should contain the following:

- brief summary of the circumstances;
- actions completed;
- arrest statement;
- victim witness statement (if taken);
- witness statement – exhibits (clothing/property);
- police property reference number;
- significant statement – comment upon arrest;
- storm log including record of first description;
- previous convictions;
- outstanding actions/lines of inquiry;
- any other relevant information or material.

The investigation plan

An investigation plan isn't simply a bullet point list of things you need to do. The purpose of the plan is to provide investigative focus, encourage a 'thinking' approach where actions and lines of inquiry are recorded with supporting rationale, and their pursuant demonstratable. While concentrating on the specific issues relevant to the case, a good investigation plan will be central to effective case management, from report to court.

The investigation plan is usually written within the first 24 hours, once any fast-track actions which might bring about an early resolution have been completed and the investigator has established what further action(s) need to be taken. How comprehensive and thorough your investigation plan will be is dependent on the type of crime you are investigating.

The demonstration of effective case management is now a feature of all investigations, even those that are considered less serious. There is now far more procedural and judicial scrutiny of the decisions we make. When a decision is made to pursue or not a line of inquiry, that decision should be capable of articulation by the investigator. A record of your decision making should provide the basis for consultation with the prosecutor, and engagement with the defence (Attorney General's Office, 2022, p 8).

The Director's Guidance issued by the Director of Public Prosecutions (the DPP) sets out the process and information required when a CPS prosecutor considers a charging decision. The Guidance makes clear that those making a request for a charging decision must provide the required information on first file submission to enable prosecutors to take decisions promptly. The request must include information as to the state of the investigation, including:

- *the reasonable lines of inquiry that have already been conducted and the results of those inquiries;*
- *the reasonable lines of inquiry which remain outstanding together with an objective assessment of the likely impact of those inquiries on the decision to charge. This should include a timescale for the completion of each inquiry and*
- *any lines of inquiry which will not be pursued and a rationale for the decision.*

(CPS, 2020, para 4.18)

It is therefore crucial that you record not just the inquiries you intend to pursue and why but importantly those that you don't intend to pursue and why. Here are some typical questions that may be asked by both a CPS prosecutor and defence.

- Why didn't you arrange for a particular digital device to be examined?
- Why didn't you submit an item for forensic analysis?
- Why didn't you undertake house-to-house inquiries?
- Why didn't you review CCTV?

These are all valid questions and ones that a prosecutor when considering a charging decision will want to know the answer to. The role of the CPS prosecutor is also to consider the evidence from the perspective of the defence. If a prosecutor identifies potential weakness in the case or matters that the defence may likely exploit, they will rightly want to understand the investigator's decision making and rationale for electing a course of action.

From the defence perspective, if you haven't completed what appears to be a reasonable and relevant line of inquiry they may seek to infer that if you had examined the digital device, completed house-to-house inquiries or reviewed the CCTV it would have proven that their client, the defendant, wasn't the person responsible for the crime. Being able to explain why you didn't pursue a line of inquiry puts the investigator in a strong position when they can demonstrate and articulate a *thinking person's* approach to their decision making.

There will always be gaps in the prosecution case where actions and inquiries haven't been pursued, whether that's because of budgets, local procedure, resource or matters outside of the investigator's control. The problem arrives where no rationale is recorded for why they weren't pursued. When this happens, the defence have free rein to suggest, for example, that the investigator selectively pursued only those inquiries that pointed towards the defendant's guilt and ignored their legal obligation and duty under CPIA to pursue inquiries that also pointed away from this.

The Investigation Management Document (IMD) provides a useful template for officers and investigators to structure their investigation plan. The CPS will request the IMD when considering a charging decision. The IMD will enhance judicial, CPS, defence and public confidence in police investigations if investigators are able to routinely explain, with reference to all the issues in the case, what they did and why, and what they did not do and why not (CPS, 2021).

Why understanding CPIA will make you a better investigator

A defendant's right to a fair trial sits at the heart of our criminal justice system where the burden of proof rests with the prosecution to prove the case beyond reasonable doubt. In this regard, the scales of justice often appear tipped in favour of the defendant where the defence simply have to introduce an element of doubt in the minds of the jury to secure an acquittal.

The onus is on the investigator to demonstrate their objectivity and independence throughout. The importance of the relationship between CPIA, the disclosure regime and the criminal justice system cannot be overstated. CPIA provides the legal and investigative framework to ensure a fair trial. It should be considered at the point where a criminal investigation commences, continue at the point of charge, and be at the forefront as the case progresses and at every subsequent court hearing (HMCPSI and HMIC, 2017).

Explore your thinking

Think about the scenario in this chapter and consider the following questions.

- In terms of importance and frequency of use in criminal investigations, how does CPIA compare against other legislation that may be relevant?

- Can you think of an offence where CPIA wouldn't feature in a criminal investigation?

- The suspect was detained and then arrested following a call from a covert officer conducting observations in the area. The subsequent investigation established that the surveillance authority, Regulation of Investigatory Powers Act 2000 (RIPA), had expired the previous day. What might be the implications for the investigation?

- Having reviewed the Police and Criminal Evidence Act (PACE) suspect interview, you notice that the suspect wasn't cautioned at the start of the interview. What might be the implications for the investigation?

Discussion

In this scenario, the prosecutor will need to decide whether the two breaches of legislation might lead to the exclusion of evidence and, if so, how might that exclusion affect the case as a whole? For example, if the suspect interview was excluded, would a fair trial still be possible and, if so, is there a realistic prospect of a conviction? If the prosecutor answers in the affirmative the case can still continue.

Unlike PACE, RIPA or other legislation in terms of frequency and importance, CPIA governs all criminal investigations and is central to ensuring a fair trial. Given this, a prosecutor or court is likely to view a breach of this legalisation far more seriously.

You read earlier about the dilemma the officer had over whether to resume and respond to emergency calls or to ask the victim of the burglary to identify property seized from the suspect. If the suspect had found the property earlier that evening, they will have been arrested and detained in a cell for several hours as an innocent person.

CPIA in some ways acts as a counterbalance to the risk of bias and assumption, and often meshes with investigative models such as the 'ABC' Rule:

- A – assume nothing;
- B – believe nothing;
- C – challenge and check everything.

In this scenario, the arresting officer came to the decision that the suspect was the person they suspected to be involved in the burglary and that they believed their arrest was necessary. However, under CPIA, as soon as that decision is made the legislation requires the arresting officer to actively consider information and material that might disprove what the officer suspects.

This is where the operational risk lies, which can challenge the integrity of an investigation when workloads are relentless and caseload leaves investigators feeling overwhelmed and the radio doesn't stop; when you know what should be done but you don't have the time. It is a common characteristic that when we feel overwhelmed and busy, we naturally look for shortcuts as we seek to relieve the load, sometimes consciously, often unconsciously.

In the context of a criminal investigation, these shortcuts often manifest in actions and lines of inquiry where investigators limit themselves to pursuing only those lines of inquiry that contribute to proving that a suspect was involved in an offence. Sometimes referred to as selective information searching, but more commonly known as confirmation bias, this is when the investigator sees only what they want to see. This mindset can have a hugely negative impact not just on the outcome of the investigation, but also on the wider criminal justice system, public opinion and the erosion of the principle of a fair trial.

Think about the scenario, about what the suspect said on arrest and your obligations under CPIA. Once it had been established that the property was stolen from the burglary, then at that time there were no other lines of inquiry to complete that may have pointed away from the suspect's guilt. However, once revealed to the suspect during their PACE interview, he changed his story and said that in fact he was with a friend who he'd met by chance shortly before his arrest and that this person had asked him to hold on to the property while he went into bushes to go to the toilet. The police arrived a short time later and he was arrested. He said that he was unaware of the burglary or that the property was stolen.

Explore your thinking

Thinking about what the suspect said, what reasonable lines of inquiry do you now need to consider to prove or disprove the suspect's involvement?

- What inquiries are you able to pursue that may point towards the suspect's involvement?

- What inquiries are you able to pursue that may point away from the suspect's involvement, or which may support or corroborate what they said in the interview?

One possible line of inquiry which you may want to pursue is to establish what the covert officer observed at or around the time of the suspect's arrest.

- Think about a situation where the covert officer observed the suspect with another person shortly before his arrest. How does this information influence your thinking?

- Think now about a situation where the covert officer had the suspect under continual observation for several minutes prior to his arrest and confirmed that he wasn't seen with another person. How does this new information influence your thinking and your decision making?

When the information and what we know changes then so might our decisions. This scenario demonstrates the need to maintain an open mind, and why adopting a *thinking person's* approach will enable you to identify lines of inquiry that aren't only reasonable and relevant but proportionate given the position of a case at a particular point in time.

Your responsibilities under CPIA remain ongoing throughout the course of the investigation, to trial and beyond. By developing a greater understanding of the principles of CPIA and disclosure and how they apply to a criminal investigation, you will be better placed to make more informed decisions which will demonstrate to others that you have complied with your duty and legal obligation under this Act.

CPIA doesn't expect or require an investigator to do the unreasonable or impossible. In conducting an investigation, the investigator should pursue all reasonable and relevant lines of inquiry, whether these point towards or away from the suspect. What is reasonable in each case will depend on the particular circumstances.

Key points

The main things for you to remember to help you make informed decisions about your approach are:

- maintain your objectivity and independence throughout – you are the fact finder not the jury;

- develop your investigative mindset – the success of a criminal investigation largely depends on the correct decision making of the investigator;

- every investigation requires an amount of investigation – the skill of the investigator is to determine which cases to build and which to bin;

- ensure defendable decision making – use the IMD to record your decisions and rationale, including why not;

- CPIA is the golden thread that runs through your investigation from report to court, and beyond.

Further reading

As an investigator you should be familiar with the Attorney General's guidelines on disclosure, which are available at: https://assets.publishing.service.gov.uk/government/uploads/system/uploads/attachment_data/file/1078194/AG_Guidelines_2022_Revision_Publication_Copy.pdf

Conclusion

This book has considered a range of different operational scenarios that you may be faced with as a PIP1 investigator. As you worked through the chapters, you may have realised that some common themes emerged.

First, it is important to make reasoned, justifiable and proportionate decisions. The decisions you make will impact:

• the quality of the investigation or incident you are managing;

• how risks are identified and managed;

• victim and witness satisfaction;

• public perception and confidence in the police;

• the legitimacy of policing;

• the core principle of policing by consent.

Secondly, the use of the national decision model can provide you with a structure to support your decision making. It can be used to support planning in an investigation as well as in live-time decision making. It is the framework against which all of your decisions are scrutinised, so you need to be familiar with it and use it.

Thirdly, your own assumptions based on your background, experiences and workplace environment can undermine objective decision making. This can lead to automatic, unthinking decisions and actions with no clear or justifiable rationale.

Fourthly, you are a professional working in a sensitive and sometimes high-risk environment. You need to think, communicate and act professionally when making decisions. This is equally true whether you are dealing with a traumatised victim, a compliant witness, an agitated or abusive member of the public or a non-compliant suspect. Your decision making needs to be fair, objective and rational whatever provocation you are faced with or whatever your personal feelings may be.

Finally, you will no doubt have realised just how many decisions are made in relation to any individual incident or investigation. This can lead to decision inertia: failing to make a decision because you may simply feel overwhelmed or not sure what to do for the best. The problem with dilemmas is that sometimes the *right* course of action isn't obvious and there are advantages and drawbacks whichever way you choose. You can't always predict the outcome of your decision and you won't always be able to please everyone with the decisions you make. However, as a professional you have a responsibility to make the difficult decisions presented by these dilemmas. Remember to follow the national decision model; gather the information, properly consider the risks, use the policy and processes to guide you and be aware of your own biases. Ensure you are able to explain and justify your decisions objectively. The importance of taking time to reflect and learn from the decisions you make is part of your continuous development and is a process that you should adopt throughout your career.

We hope you have enjoyed the book and it has given you some information and ideas that you can embed in your real-world practice.

References

Aarts, H and Dijksterhuis, A (2000) Habits as Knowledge Structures: Automaticity in Goal-Directed Behavior. *Journal of Personality and Social Psychology*, 78(1): 53–63.

Atkinson, D (2018) Suffragettes and the British Museum. [online] Available at: www. britishmuseum.org/blog/suffragettes-and-british-museum (accessed 9 June 2023).

Attorney General's Office (2022) *Attorney General's Guidelines on Disclosure: For Investigators, Prosecutors and Defence Practitioners*. [online] Available at: https://assets.publishing.service.gov.uk/government/uploads/system/uploads/attachment_data/file/1078194/AG_Guidelines_2022_Revision_Publication_Copy.pdf (accessed 24 April 2023).

Baber, M and Jeffs, H (1996) *Stalking, Harassment and Intimidation and the Protection from Harassment Bill*. Research Paper 96/115. London: House of Commons Library.

Bandura, A (1971) *Social Learning Theory*. New York: General Learning Press.

Bank Mellat v HM Treasury (No. 2) [2013] UKSC39. [online] Available at: www.bailii.org/uk/cases/UKSC/2013/39.html (accessed 9 June 2023).

Britain Thinks (2019) *Crimes Against Older People: Research Commissioned by Her Majesty's Inspectorate of Constabulary and Fire & Rescue Services*. [online] Available at: www.justiceinspectorates.gov.uk/hmicfrs/wp-content/uploads/crimes-against-older-people-research.pdf (accessed 31 March 2023).

Brown, J and Mead, D (2021) *Police Powers: Protest*. Briefing Paper No. 5013. London: House of Commons Library.

Caluori, J (2021) No Right Move? Devolving Decision Making for Criminally Exploited Children. [online] Available at: www.crestadvisory.com/post/no-right-move-devolving-decision-making-for-criminally-exploited-children (accessed 2 May 2023).

Centrex (2005) *Practice Advice on Core Investigative Doctrine*. Cambridgeshire: NCPE.

College of Policing (2013) National Decision Model. [online] Available at: www.college.police.uk/app/national-decision-model/national-decision-model (accessed 9 June 2023).

College of Policing (2014) *Code of Ethics*. Coventry: College of Policing.

College of Policing (2019) Briefing Note: For Police First Responders to a Report of Rape or Sexual Assault. [online] Available at: https://library.college.police.uk/docs/appref/C909E0418-First-Responders-Brief.pdf (accessed 20 April 2023).

College of Policing (2021) Risk and Associated Investigations. [online] Available at: www.college.police.uk/app/major-investigation-and-public-protection/investigating-child-abuse-and-safeguarding-children/police-response-investigating-child-abuse/risk-and-associated-investigations (accessed 2 May 2023).

College of Policing (2023) Investigation Process. [online] Available at: www.college.police.uk/app/investigation/investigation-process (accessed 24 April 2023).

Cook, T and Tattersall, A (2014) *Senior Investigating Officers' Handbook*. Oxford: Oxford University Press.

Criminal Justice Joint Inspection (CJJI) (2021) Evaluation of Rape Survivors' Experience of the Police & Other Criminal Justice Agencies. [online] Available at: www.justiceinspectorates.gov.uk/hmicfrs/publication-html/evaluation-of-rape-survivors-experience-of-police-and-other-criminal-justice-agencies (accessed 20 April 2023).

Criminal Justice Joint Inspection (CJJI) (2022) Criminal Justice System Continues to Fail Rape Victims. [online] Available at: www.justiceinspectorates.gov.uk/hmicfrs/news/news-feed/criminal-justice-system-continues-to-fail-rape-victims (accessed 20 April 2023).

Criminal Procedure and Investigations Act 1996. [online] Available at: www.legislation.gov.uk/ukpga/1996/25/contents (accessed 9 June 2023).

Crown Prosecution Service (CPS) (2018) Stalking and Harassment. [online] Available at: www.cps.gov.uk/legal-guidance/stalking-and-harassment (accessed 9 June 2023).

Crown Prosecution Service (CPS) (2020) Charging (The Director's Guidance) – sixth edition, December 2020, incorporating the National File Standard. [online] Available at: www.cps.gov.uk/legal-guidance/charging-directors-guidance-sixth-edition-december-2020-incorporating-national-file (accessed 24 April 2023).

Crown Prosecution Service (CPS) (2021) National Disclosure Improvement Plan (NDIP) Report on Phase Two – March 2021. [online] Available at: www.cps.gov.uk/publication/national-disclosure-improvement-plan-ndip-report-phase-two-march-2021 (accessed 24 April 2023).

Crown Prosecution Service (CPS) (2022a) Modern Slavery, Human Trafficking and Smuggling. [online] Available at: www.cps.gov.uk/legal-guidance/modern-slavery-human-trafficking-and-smuggling (accessed 2 May 2023).

Crown Prosecution Service (CPS) (2022b) Disclosure Manual: Chapter 5 – Reasonable Lines of Enquiry and Third Parties. [online] Available at: www.cps.gov.uk/legal-guidance/disclosure-manual-chapter-5-reasonable-lines-enquiry-and-third-parties (accessed 24 April 2023).

Crown Prosecution Service (CPS) (nd) Statements Obtained Over the Telephone: Best Practice Guidance. [online] Available at: www.cps.gov.uk/sites/default/files/documents/legal_guidance/Telephone-Statements-Best-Practice-Guidance.pdf (accessed 31 March 2023).

Field, F, Miller, M and Butler-Sloss, E (2019) *Independent Review of the Modern Slavery Act 2015: Final Report*. [online] Available at: https://assets.publishing.service.gov.uk/government/uploads/system/uploads/attachment_data/file/803406/Independent_review_of_the_Modern_Slavery_Act_-_final_report.pdf (accessed 2 May 2023).

Gammon, M and Easton, J (2019) *Disproportionality in the Youth Justice System*. [online] Available at: www.magistrates-association.org.uk/Portals/0/Disproportionality%20in%20the%20youth%20justice%20system_MA%20report_August%202019.pdf (accessed 2 May 2023).

Gekoski, A, Massey, K, Allen, K, Ferreira, J, Dalton, C T, Horvarth, M and Davies, K (2023) 'A Lot of the Time It's Dealing with Victims Who Don't Want to Know, It's All Made Up, or They've Got Mental Health': Rape Myths in a Large English Police Force. *International Review of Victimology*: 1–22.

Havard, T (2022) *Serious Youth Violence: County Lines Drug Dealing and the Government Response*. [online] Available at: https://researchbriefings.files.parliament.uk/documents/CBP-9264/CBP-9264.pdf (accessed 2 May 2023).

Hethmon, H (2020) Revolt: The Story of England's First Protest. [online] Available at: https://media.nationalarchives.gov.uk/index.php/revolt-story-englands-first-protest (accessed 9 June 2023).

HM Government (2016) *Ending Gang Violence and Exploitation*. [online] Available at: https://assets.publishing.service.gov.uk/government/uploads/system/uploads/attachment_data/file/491699/Ending_gang_violence_and_Exploitation_FINAL.pdf (accessed 2 May 2023).

HM Government (2021) *The End-to-End Rape Review Report on Findings and Actions*. [online] Available at: https://assets.publishing.service.gov.uk/government/uploads/system/uploads/attachment_data/file/1001417/end-to-end-rape-review-report-with-correction-slip.pdf (accessed 20 April 2023).

HMCPSI and HMIC (2017) *Making It Fair: A Joint Inspection of the Disclosure of Unused Material in Volume Crown Court Cases*. [online] Available at: www.justiceinspectorates.gov.uk/cjji/wp-content/uploads/sites/2/2017/07/CJJI_DSC_thm_July17_rpt.pdf (accessed 24 April 2023).

HMCPSI and HMICFRS (2019) *The Poor Relation: The Police and Crown Prosecution Service's Response to Crimes Against Older People*. [online] Available at: www.justiceinspectorates.gov.uk/hmicfrs/publication-html/crimes-against-older-people (accessed 31 March 2023).

HMIC (2017) *Living in Fear – the Police and CPS Response to Harassment and Stalking: A Joint Inspection by HMIC and HMCPSI*. [online] Available at: www.justiceinspectorates.gov.uk/hmicfrs/wp-content/uploads/living-in-fear-the-police-and-cps-response-to-harassment-and-stalking.pdf (accessed 9 June 2023).

HMICFRS (2021a) *Disproportionate Use of Police Powers: A Spotlight on Stop and Search and the Use of Force*. [online] Available at: https://crimeline.co.uk/wp-content/uploads/2021/02/disproportionate-use-of-police-powers-spotlight-on-stop-search-and-use-of-force.pdf (accessed 9 June 2023).

HMICFRS (2021b) *Getting the Balance Right? An Inspection of How Effectively the Police Deal with Protests*. [online] Available at: www.justiceinspectorates.gov.uk/hmicfrs/wp-content/uploads/getting-the-balance-right-an-inspection-of-how-effectively-the-police-deal-with-protests.pdf (accessed 9 June 2023).

HMICFRS (2021c) A *Joint Thematic Inspection of the Police and Crown Prosecution Service's Response to Rape – Phase One: From Report to Police or CPS Decision to Take No Further Action*. [online] Available at: www.justiceinspectorates.gov.uk/hmicfrs/publication-html/a-joint-thematic-inspection-of-the-police-and-crown-prosecution-services-response-to-rape-phase-one (accessed 20 April 2023).

Home Office (2012) Circular: A Change to the Protection from Harassment Act 1997: Circular 018/ 2012. [online] Available at: www.gov.uk/government/publications/a-change-to-the-protection-from-harassment-act-1997-introduction-of-two-new-specific-offences-of-stalking (accessed 9 June 2023).

Home Office (2018) Criminal Exploitation of Children and Vulnerable Adults: County Lines Guidance. [online] Available at: https://assets.publishing.service.gov.uk/government/uploads/system/uploads/attachment_data/file/863323/HOCountyLinesGuidance_-_Sept2018.pdf (accessed 2 May 2023).

Home Office (2021) *Stalking Protection Orders: Statutory Guidance for the Police*. [online] Available at: https://assets.publishing.service.gov.uk/government/uploads/system/uploads/attachment_data/file/951354/SPOs_statutory_guidance_English_with_changes__002_.pdf (accessed 9 June 2023).

Home Office (2022a) *Police Powers and Procedures: Stop and Search and Arrests, England and Wales, Year Ending 31 March 2021 Second Edition*. [online] Available at: www.gov.uk/government/statistics/police-powers-and-procedures-stop-and-search-and-arrests-england-and-wales-year-ending-31-march-2021/police-powers-and-procedures-stop-and-search-and-arrests-england-and-wales-year-ending-31-march-2021 (accessed 2 October 2022).

Home Office (2022b) Modern Slavery: National Referral Mechanism and Duty to Notify Statistics, UK Quarter 3 2022 – July to September. [online] Available at: www.gov.uk/government/statistics/national-referral-mechanism-and-duty-to-notify-statistics-uk-july-to-september-2022/modern-slavery-national-referral-mechanism-and-duty-to-notify-statistics-uk-quarter-3-2022-july-to-september (accessed 2 May 2023).

Home Office (2023) National Referral Mechanism Guidance: Adult (England and Wales). [online] Available at: www.gov.uk/government/publications/human-trafficking-victims-referral-and-assessment-forms/guidance-on-the-national-referral-mechanism-for-potential-adult-victims-of-modern-slavery-england-and-wales (accessed 2 May 2023).

Horwell, R (2017) *Mouncher Investigation Report*. [online] Available at: https://assets.publishing.service.gov.uk/government/uploads/system/uploads/attachment_data/file/629725/mouncher_report_web_accessible_july_2017.pdf (accessed 24 April 2023).

Independent Anti-Slavery Commissioner (2020) IASC Call for Evidence: Use of the Modern Slavery Act's Section 45 Statutory Defence. [online] Available at: www.antislaverycommissioner.co.uk/news-insights/closed-iasc-call-for-evidence-use-of-the-modern-slavery-act-s-section-45-statutory-defence (accessed 2 May 2023).

Independent Office for Police Conduct (IOPC) (2018) *Shana Grice: Investigation into Sussex Police Contact with Shana Grice Prior to Her Murder on 25 August 2016*. [online] Available at: www.policeconduct.gov.uk/sites/default/files/Shana%20Grice_Final_report_for_publication.pdf (accessed 9 June 2023).

Independent Office for Police Conduct (IOPC) (2022a) *National Stop and Search Learning Report*. London: IOPC.

Independent Office for Police Conduct (IOPC) (2022b) Hertfordshire Officers Given Final Written Warnings over Contact with Christie Frewin Prior to Her Murder. [online] Available at: www.policeconduct.gov.uk/news/hertfordshire-officers-given-final-written-warnings-over-contact-christie-frewin-prior-her (accessed 9 June 2023).

Innes, M, Brookman, F and Jones, H (2021) "Mosaicking": Cross Construction, Sense-making and Methods of Police Investigation. *Policing: An International Journal of Police Strategies and Management*, 44(4): 708–21.

James, E (2021) *Exploited and Criminalised*. [online] Available at: www.barnardos.org.uk/sites/default/files/2021-10/Exploited%20and%20Criminalised%20report.pdf (accessed 2 May 2023).

Kent Police (2021) Crime and Intelligence – Taking Statements. [online] Available at: www.kent.police.uk/foi-ai/kent-police/Policy/crime-and-intelligence/police-response-to-victims-and-witnesses-referring-to-extended-victim-services-in-kent-n15b (accessed 31 March 2023).

Levine, P A (1997) *Waking the Tiger: Healing Trauma*. Berkeley, CA: North Atlantic Books.

Llwyd, E (2012) *Independent Parliamentary Inquiry into Stalking Law Reform*. London: Justice Unions' Parliamentary Group.

Lodrick, Z (2007) Psychological Trauma – What Every Trauma Worker Should Know. *The British Journal of Psychotherapy Integration*, 4(2): 1–19.

Maher, R (2014) The Peterloo Massacre. [online] Available at: www.bl.uk/romantics-and-victorians/articles/the-peterloo-massacre (accessed 9 June 2023).

Martellozzo, E, Bleakley, P, Bradbury, P, Frost, S and Short, E (2022) Police Responses to Cyberstalking during the Covid-19 Pandemic in the UK. *The Police Journal: Theory, Practice and Principles*. [online] Available at: https://eprints.mdx.ac.uk/35314 (accessed 9 June 2023).

McKeon, B, McEwan, T E and Luebbers, S (2015) "It's Not Really Stalking If You Know the Person": Measuring Community Attitudes That Normalize, Justify and Minimise Stalking. *Psychiatry, Psychology and Law*, 22(2): 291–306.

McLean, F, Meakins, A and White, E (2022) Conducting Effective Investigations: Rapid Evidence Assessment. [online] Available at: https://assets.college.police.uk/s3fs-public/2022-07/Conducting-effective-investigations-rapid-evidence-assessment.pdf (accessed 24 April 2023).

Ministry of Justice (2020) *Code of Practice for Victims of Crime in England and Wales*. [online] Available at: https://assets.publishing.service.gov.uk/government/uploads/system/uploads/attachment_data/file/974376/victims-code-2020.pdf (accessed 31 March 2023).

Ministry of Justice (2022) *Achieving Best Evidence in Criminal Proceedings: Guidance on Interviewing Victims and Witnesses, and Guidance on Using Special Measures*. [online] Available at: www.gov.uk/government/publications/achieving-best-evidence-in-criminal-proceedings (accessed: 31 March 2023).

Monckton-Smith, J, Szymanska, K and Haile, S (2004) *Exploring the Relationship between Stalking and Homicide*. [online] Available at: https://eprints.glos.ac.uk/4553 (accessed 9 June 2023).

National Crime Agency (NCA) (2019) *County Lines Drug Supply, Vulnerability and Harm 2018*. [online] Available at: www.nationalcrimeagency.gov.uk/who-we-are/publications/257-county-lines-drug-supply-vulnerability-and-harm-2018/file (accessed 9 June 2023).

National Crime Agency (NCA) (2020) *National Strategic Assessment of Serious and Organised Crime*. [online] Available at: www.nationalcrimeagency.gov.uk/who-we-are/publications/437-national-strategic-assessment-of-serious-and-organised-crime-2020/file (accessed 2 May 2023).

National Police Chiefs' Council (NPCC) (2015) *Policing Vision 2025*. [online] Available at: https://assets.college.police.uk/s3fs-public/policing_vision_2025.pdf (accessed 18 April 2023).

National Police Chiefs' Council (NPCC) (2022) *Body-Worn Video*. [online] Available at: www.npcc.police.uk/SysSiteAssets/media/downloads/publications/publications-log/2022/body-worn-video-guidance.pdf (accessed 20 April 2023).

National Police Chiefs' Council (NPCC) and Crown Prosecution Service (CPS) (2018) *Protocol on the Appropriate Handling of Stalking or Harassment Offences between the National Police Chiefs' Council and the Crown Prosecution Service*. London: NPCC and CPS.

Nickolls, L and Allen, G (2022) *Police Powers: Stop and Search (Number SN03878)*. London: House of Commons Library.

Office for National Statistics (ONS) (2022a) Stalking: Findings from the Crime Survey for England and Wales (CSEW) Year Ending March 2022. [online] Available at: www.ons.gov.uk/peoplepopulationand community/crimeandjustice/datasets/stalkingfindingsfromthecrimesurveyforenglandandwales (accessed 9 June 2023).

Office for National Statistics (ONS) (2022b) Crime in England and Wales: Year Ending June 2022. [online] Available at: www.ons.gov.uk/peoplepopulationandcommunity/crimeandjustice/bulletins/crimeinenglandandwales/yearendingjune2022 (accessed 20 April 2023).

Oxford Dictionaries (2013) *Pocket Oxford English Dictionary*. Oxford: Oxford University Press.

Police Foundation (2009) Stalking and Harassment. *The Briefing*, 1(6): 1–12.

Rape Crisis (2002) The 5 Fs: Fight, Flight, Freeze, Flop and Friend. [online] Available at: https://rapecrisis.org.uk/get-help/tools-for-victims-and-survivors/understanding-your-response/fight-or-flight (accessed 20 April 2023).

Riddell, F (2018) Suffragettes, Violence and Militancy. [online] Available at: www.bl.uk/votes-for-women/articles/suffragettes-violence-and-militancy (accessed 10 December 2022).

Scarman, L G (1981) *The Scarman Report: The Brixton Disorders 10–12 April 1981: Report of an Inquiry*. London: HMSO.

Scott, A J and Sheridan, L (2011) 'Reasonable' Perceptions of Stalking: The Influence of Conduct Severity and the Perpetrator–Target Relationship. *Psychology, Crime and Law*, 17(4): 331–44.

Stone, V and Pettigrew, P (2000) *The Views of the Public on Stops and Searches (Police Research Series Paper Number 129).* London: Home Office.

Strand, S and McEwan, T E (2012) Violence among Female Stalkers. *Psychological Medicine*, 42: 545–55.

Suzy Lamplugh Trust (2022) Super-complaint on the Police Response to Stalking. [online] Available at: www.suzylamplugh.org/Handlers/Download.ashx?IDMF=cf3fdc8b-f958-4cc0-9fc7-9ce6de3e9137 (accessed 9 June 2023).

Tiratelli, M, Quinton, P and Bradford, B (2018) Does Stop and Search Deter Crime? Evidence from Ten Years of London-wide Data. *British Journal of Criminology*, 58: 1212–31.

Tyler, T R (2003) Procedural Justice, Legitimacy, and the Effective Rule of Law. In Tonry, M (ed) *Crime and Justice: A Review of Research* (pp 431–505). London: The University of Chicago Press.

United Nations (2022) Universal Declaration of Human Rights. [online] Available at: www.un.org/en/about-us/universal-declaration-of-human-rights (accessed 9 June 2023).

Windle, J, Moyle, L and Coomber, R (2020) 'Vulnerable' Kids Going Country: Children and Young People's Involvement in County Lines Drug Dealing. *Youth Justice*, 20(1–2): 64–78.

World Health Organization (2012) Understanding and Addressing Violence Against Women: Sexual Violence. [online] Available at: https://apps.who.int/iris/bitstream/handle/10665/77434/WHO_RHR_12.37_eng.pdf (accessed 2 May 2023).

Index

For Product Safety Concerns and Information please contact our EU
representative GPSR@taylorandfrancis.com
Taylor & Francis Verlag GmbH, Kaufingerstraße 24, 80331 München, Germany

www.ingramcontent.com/pod-product-compliance
Lightning Source LLC
Chambersburg PA
CBHW061752270326
41928CB00011B/2477